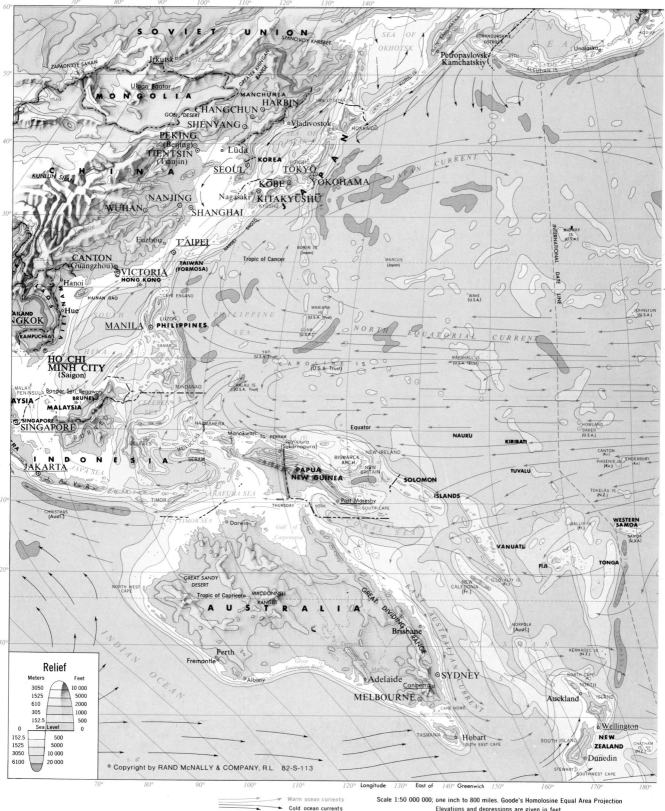

SOVIET UNION

ZAPADNYYE SAYAN
Irkutsk
Lake Baikal
STANOVOY KHREBET
SEA OF OKHOTSK

Ulaan Baatar
MONGOLIA
CHANGCHUN
SHENYANG
GOBI DESERT
MANCHURIA
HARBIN
GREATER KHINGAN RANGE
Vladivostok
HOKKAIDO

Petropavlovsk-Kamchatskiy
KOMANDORSKIYE OSTROVA
ATTU
ALEUTIAN IS.
Unalaska
Aqdiak
ALASKA

PEKING
(Beijing)
TIENTSIN
(Tianjin)
Lüda
HONSHU
SEOUL
KOREA
TOKYO
KŌBE
YOKOHAMA
Nagasaki
KITAKYUSHU
KYŪSHŪ
JAPAN CURRENT

KUNLUN SHAN
CHINA
NANJING
WUHAN
SHANGHAI
Fuzhou
T'AIPEI
NANSEI SHOTO
BONIN IS. (Japan)
MARCUS (Japan)
MIDWAY IS. (U.S.A.)
INTERNATIONAL DATE LINE

CANTON
(Guangzhou)
VICTORIA
HONG KONG (Br.)
Hanoi
TAIWAN (FORMOSA)
Tropic of Cancer
HAINAN DAO
CAPE ENGANO
WAKE (U.S.A.)
JOHNSTON (U.S.A.)

THAILAND
BANGKOK
LAOS
Hue
VIETNAM
SOUTH CHINA SEA
LUZON
PHILIPPINE SEA
MARIANA IS. (U.S.A. Trust)
GUAM (U.S.A.)
NORTH EQUATORIAL CURRENT

MANILA
PHILIPPINES
SAMAR
YAP (U.S.A. Trust)
CAROLINE IS.
MARSHALL IS. (U.S.A. Trust)

KAMPUCHEA
HO CHI MINH CITY
(Saigon)
MINDANAO
PALAU IS. (U.S.A. Trust)

MALAY PENINSULA
Bandar Seri Begawan
BRUNEI (Br.)
MALAYSIA
CELEBES SEA
HALMAHERA
Manokwari
TG. PERRAM
NEW IRELAND
NAURU
KIRIBATI
HOWLAND BAKER (U.S.A.)
CANTON
PHOENIX IS. (Kir.)
ENDERBURY (Kir.)

SINGAPORE
BORNEO
CELEBES
MOLUCCAS
SERAM
Djayapura
(Sukarnapura)
BISMARCK ARCH.
NEW BRITAIN
SOLOMON ISLANDS
TUVALU
TOKELAU IS. (N.Z.)

JAKARTA
JAVA SEA
INDONESIA
Equator
PAPUA NEW GUINEA
TRENCH
Port Moresby
SOUTH CAPE
WALLIS IS. (Fr.)
WESTERN SAMOA
SAMOA (U.S.A.)

CHRISTMAS (Austl.)
TIMOR
ARAFURA SEA
TIMOR SEA
Darwin
THURSDAY CAPE YORK
Gulf of Carpentaria
CORAL SEA
VANUATU
NEW CALEDONIA (Fr.)
LOYALTY IS. (Fr.)
FIJI
TONGA

GREAT SANDY DESERT
NORTH WEST CAPE
Tropic of Capricorn
MACDONNELL RANGES
AUSTRALIA
GREAT DIVIDING RANGE
EAST AUSTRALIAN CURRENT
Brisbane
NORFOLK (Austl.)

Perth
Fremantle
Great Australian Bight
Albany
Adelaide
Canberra
SYDNEY
MELBOURNE
CAPE HOWE
Bass Strait
KERMADEC IS. (N.Z.)
NORTH CAPE
NORTH ISLAND
Auckland

INDIAN OCEAN

TASMANIA
Hobart
SOUTH EAST CAPE
SOUTH ISLAND
NEW ZEALAND
Wellington
CHATHAM IS. (N.Z.)
Dunedin
STEWART
SOUTHWEST CAPE

Relief

Meters	Feet
3050	10 000
1525	5000
610	2000
305	1000
152.5	500
0	Sea Level	0
152.5	500
1525	5000
3050	10 000
6100	20 000

© Copyright by RAND McNALLY & COMPANY, R.L. 82-S-113

Longitude   East of   Greenwich

Warm ocean currents
Cold ocean currents

Scale 1:50 000 000; one inch to 800 miles. Goode's Homolosine Equal Area Projection
Elevations and depressions are given in feet

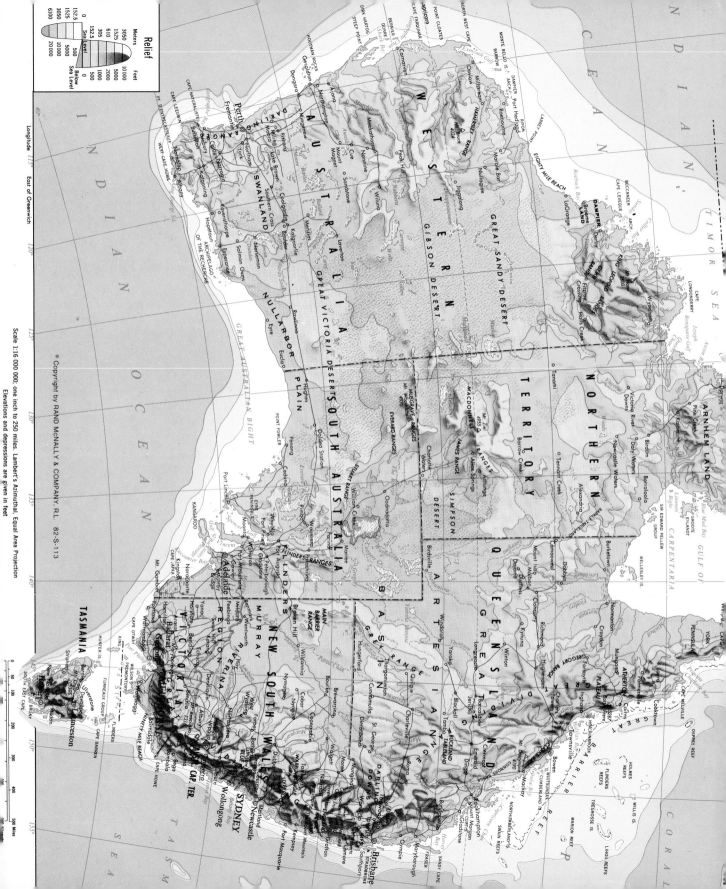

Enchantment of the World

AUSTRALIA

By Emilie U. Lepthien

Consultants; The Australian Information Services and the library staff of the Australian Consulate-General, New York City and Pamela J. Griffiths Clark, M.L.S., University of New South Wales, Sydney

Consultant for Social Studies; Donald W. Nylin, Ph.D., Assistant Superintendent for Instruction, Aurora West Public Schools, Aurora, Illinois

Consultant for Reading; Robert L. Hillerich, Ph.D., Bowling Green State University, Bowling Green Ohio

CHILDRENS PRESS, CHICAGO

A volcanic crater lake in South Australia

To my parents Agnes and Henry Utteg

Library of Congress Cataloging in Publication Data

Lepthien, Emilie Utteg.
  Australia.

  (Enchantment of the world)
  Includes index.
  Summary: Introduces the history, geography,
geology, industries, animals, Aboriginals,
tourist attractions, and other aspects of
Australia today.
    1. Australia—Description and travel—
1981- —Juvenile literature. 2. Australia
—History—Juvenile literature. [1. Australia]
I. Title. II. Series.
DU105.2.L46 1982   994   82-4541
ISBN 0-516-02751-4   AACR2

Picture Acknowledgments
Colour Library International: cover, pages 4, 5, 6, 8, 11, 15,
16, 21, 23, 27, 29, 41, 43, 44, 51 (top and bottom), 56, 58, 60
(2 photos), 61 (2 photos), 62, 64, 70, 74, 79, 81, 82, 85, 89,
93, 98, 100, 104 (2 photos), 106, 107, 108, 115
Australian Information Service: pages 13, 14, 30, 32, 34,
35, 37, 39, 47, 48 (2 photos), 53, 54, 55, 66, 68, 72, 76, 78, 86,
91, 96, 101, 112
Len W. Meents: maps on pages 24 and 75 and all spot
maps
James P. Rowan: pages 40 and 52
Emilie U. Lepthien: page 51 (center)
Australian Postal Commision: page 36
Brookfield Zoo: page 46
Hillstrom Stock Photos—Jane Shepstone: page 19
**Courtesy Flag Research Center, Winchester,
Massachusetts 01890:** flag on back cover
Cover: Sydney Harbor Bridge viewed from the passenger
terminal in Sydney Harbor

The waters of Bass Strait, which separate mainland Australia from Tasmania, have carved strange shapes in the coastline.

TABLE OF CONTENTS

Bilgola, a beach in Sydney, New South Wales

Chapter 1

AUSTRALIA—THE UNIQUE CONTINENT

Not only is Australia a country, it is an island large enough to be called a continent. The name comes from the Latin word *australis,* which means "south" or "south wind." No other country in the world occupies an entire continent.

About A.D. 150, the Greek philosopher Ptolemy suggested that a landmass must exist south of Asia. He believed there was land at the North Pole. So there would have to be land to balance it at the bottom of the world. He called this land *Terra Australis Incognita,* the Unknown Southern Land.

Many centuries later, men discovered there was no land at the North Pole. But there were great landmasses far south of the Equator. These two continents are now called Australia and Antarctica.

Australia is truly unique. It is the oldest, smallest, and flattest continent. Some scientists believe that millions of years ago it was part of a supercontinent called Gondwanaland. Parts of Gondwanaland broke off and drifted slowly northward. Separate continents, islands, and other landmasses were formed.

Except for Antarctica, Australia was the last continent to be discovered and explored. In 1607 European sailors first landed on Australia's shores. But they were not the first humans to arrive. The Aboriginals had come at least forty thousand years before.

Aboriginals, the first inhabitants of Australia

THE FIRST INHABITANTS

In school, children learn that scientists cannot agree where the Aboriginals came from or how they traveled. There might have been land bridges from the north. Maybe island stepping-stones enabled people to come from Indonesia, Sri Lanka, India, or Malaysia by raft or canoe.

THE UNIQUE TERRAIN

Australia is not only the flattest continent, it is also the lowest in altitude. Its average height above sea level is only 1,000 feet (304.8 meters). The Great Dividing Range is only a short distance inland from the Pacific Ocean. It is not a high mountain range. But it is responsible for the arid land to the west. The trade winds blow in from the Coral and Tasman seas. They lose their moisture on the eastern slopes of the mountains.

In this narrow belt between the seashore and the mountains the soil is fertile and rain is plentiful. Farms produce great quantities of meat, fruits, and vegetables. The chief cities of Australia are located along the east coast, especially in the southeast. Many people who live there never have visited the great outback (the interior) beyond the mountains.

West of the mountains stretches a vast tableland. In this part of the outback, rain and irrigation support crops, cattle, and sheep. Still farther west are the great deserts. They cover one third of the continent. Sheep and cattle stations cover thousands of acres. The people who own or manage these stations often live more than 100 miles (160.9 kilometers) from their nearest neighbors.

Another fertile band with enough rain for grazing and crops is along the shores of the Indian Ocean on the southwestern coast.

THE AUSSIES

The British first settled on the continent in 1788. They brought their language, customs, and way of life. Today that life-style—housing, food, clothing, industry, and culture—reminds visitors and new residents of life in western Europe and North America.

The Commonwealth of Australia is an independent nation. It is freely associated with Great Britain. The prime minister is leader of the Australian government. Queen Elizabeth II is also queen of Australia. As head of state, the queen is represented by the governor-general and six state governors. The queen appoints these representatives on the recommendation of elected state and federal governmental bodies.

English is the official language. But the Australians (or Aussies, as they are called) have developed their own accent. They also use many interesting words and phrases.

An Aussie may tell someone to "give it a burl, cobber." He really is saying, "Try it, friend." Each year almost three quarters of a million people do try Australia, moving there for business or vacations. They find a new life in a young country.

ENJOYING AUSTRALIA

Visitors should remember that when it's summer north of the equator it's winter "down under." Even so the Australian winter from June to August is usually pleasant near the coast. Snow falls in the Australian Alps, part of the Great Dividing Range. Skiing is a popular sport in winter. The northernmost peninsula is in the Torrid Zone, north of the Tropic of Capricorn. There the climate is tropical all year.

Aussies enjoy sports. The climate is ideal for playing various sports throughout the year. They like soccer, lawn bowling, tennis, golf, cricket, archery, cycling, and rugby. Those who live near the coast go sailing, swimming, and deep-sea fishing. They travel to the Great Barrier Reef. Here are the beautiful coral islands off the continent's Pacific coast. It is a paradise of

Palm trees grow in the warmer coastal areas of Australia.

underwater marine life. It delights skin and scuba divers and photographers. Those who walk over these islands find the coral to be razor sharp. They must wear strong shoes.

People who live on cattle and sheep stations in the outback enjoy the wide open spaces. They often feel uncomfortable in crowded cities. Their trips to town, sometimes by private plane, are infrequent.

A LONG WAY FROM ALMOST EVERYWHERE

Australia is a long distance from the major industrial cities of the world. New Guinea lies just across the Torres Strait north of Cape York. The islands of Indonesia are north of Darwin across the Timor Sea. Australia's nearest industrialized neighbor is New Zealand.

Jets fly from the West Coast of the United States. They refuel in Honolulu, Tahiti, or Fiji on the long flight to Sydney. It is an exciting experience to cross the international date line. Heading west, travelers "lose" a day. Flying east they gain a day.

UNIQUE ANIMALS IN A UNIQUE LAND

Isolated from other continents, Australia's native animal life is unique. Many of the native animals are marsupials. A marsupial is a mammal whose female carries her young in a pouch after they are born.

The koala, kangaroo, and wallaby are the most famous of the country's marsupials. But there are more than one hundred different species of pouched animals. They range in size from the 7-foot (2.1 meters) tall kangaroo to the smallest insect-eating marsupial the size of a mouse. A newborn kangaroo is only 1 inch (25 millimeters) long. It climbs into its mother's pouch. Here it nurses until it is old enough to find food.

The dingo is generally believed to have evolved from a domesticated version of the Asiatic wolf and Indian wild dog brought to the continent by ancestral Aboriginals. They used the wild dogs to help them hunt. Today dingoes roam the countryside and kill unprotected sheep and cattle. The government has built

Kangaroos hold their short forelegs down in front when they are resting.

The Aboriginals used dingoes to help them hunt.

the longest fence in the world. It protects sheep and cattle stations from these wild dogs. The Dingo Fence encloses one third of the country. It is kept in repair through constant patrolling.

Rabbits and foxes also were brought into the country. They, too, have become nuisances. Rabbits became so numerous that the Rabbit Fence was built. It stretches between the Indian Ocean and the southern shore. Other protective measures have greatly reduced the rabbit problem. The precious grass is being protected for the cattle and sheep.

Part of the Great Sandy Desert

AUSTRALIA'S UNIQUE RED CENTER

The "red center" covers the middle of the continent. It is miles and miles of desert. Alice Springs is in the heart of the red center. It might be considered an oasis in the desert.

AUSTRALIA'S UNIQUE CAPITAL

Canberra is the country's newest major city. It is the seat of the Commonwealth government. It is also a major center of education and research.

Australia is a very new nation with a very short history. It is also a continent with a very long history. Its people are proud, hardworking, and friendly. If someone should invite you for a visit "down under," be sure to "give it a burl, cobber."

The outdoors served as a classroom for the Aboriginals.

Chapter 2

PEOPLE FROM
OUT OF THE PAST

For more than forty thousand years Aboriginal children have gone to school. The whole outdoors served as their classroom. Parents and tribal elders knew that survival in a hostile environment depended on the lessons they taught.

As nomads, the Aboriginals roamed the deserts, semideserts, and woodlands of the continent. Until very recent times, these Stone Age people lived as hunters and food gatherers. They built no permanent homes and did no farming. They had no herds of animals. Most of their time was spent in locating water, gathering food, and building temporary shelters.

DREAMTIME

Aboriginal children also were taught the myths and religious customs of the tribe. These myths about Dreamtime still are handed down.

Dreamtime was the period in which the First People lived. The First People were spirits that lived long before the tribes. The Aboriginals believed these spirits were responsible for all natural wonders—sea, sun, stars, rain, and fire. Landforms were marks left by their ancestors that held their spirits. Today these landmarks still designate tribal boundaries. On the highway north of Alice Springs are huge granite boulders. They are called the Devil's Marbles. The Aboriginals say they are eggs laid by the mythical Rainbow Snake in Dreamtime.

WANDERERS IN DESERT AND HIGHLAND

More than five hundred tribes inhabited the continent. Each respected the territory of tribes around it. The Aboriginal population was estimated at about three hundred thousand when European sailors discovered the land.

Each tribe had its own dialect. The tribes could communicate through hand signals and similarities in their speech. The Aboriginal languages differ completely from languages anywhere else in the world.

As nomads, the clans seldom spent more than two or three days in one place. The fifty to seventy people in each clan had to be fed. So the members had to keep on the move.

At times they were conservationists. The women gathered berries, nuts, birds' eggs, and grass seeds. Using digging sticks they uncovered wild yams, grubs, and snails. The women taught young girls how to gather food. They warned them not to take all of the eggs or gather all of the seeds or dig up all of the yams. Some had to be left if there was to be food the next year.

The men used spears and spear-throwers (woomera) and boomerangs for hunting. (A boomerang is a curved implement that returns to its starting point if thrown properly.) The boomerangs were only slightly curved. The Aboriginals could throw them with deadly aim. Curved, returning boomerangs were

Aboriginal children

lighter in weight. They were used mostly for sport or to frighten flocks of birds. Some tribes also used clubs. They fastened stones to the ends of strong sticks with kangaroo sinew. These simple weapons were used to kill kangaroos, emus, wombats, and smaller animals.

SPECIAL CEREMONIES

Initiation for the Aboriginal boy took longer than did that of a girl. It was very hard. The men of the clan had to make sure the boy could live under the most difficult circumstances. Major initiation rites could begin when a boy was eight years old. They might continue throughout his life. One member of the clan was chosen to supervise the instruction. At times during the long initiation period a corroboree or ceremonial dance was held. This honored the boy as he reached another stage in growth toward manhood. Other clans in the tribe were invited to the ceremony.

Corroborees began after nightfall following a feast. Sometimes they celebrated a good hunt and told the story of a legendary hero of Dreamtime or imitated the behavior of birds and animals.

Usually only the men danced. They kept time to the strange, deep notes from the didgeridoo, a hollowed-out tree branch. The man blowing it set the beat for the dance. The women sat in the background. They watched and hummed as the men danced in the light of bonfires. The men in the corroboree decorated themselves with paint and sometimes feathers.

ON THE MOVE

The small clans moved from place to place searching for food and water. The men carried their few possessions—spears, woomeras, and boomerangs. They left behind for future use any simple tools they had made at a site. The boys carried smaller weapons. They helped in the hunt.

The women balanced large, bowl-shaped dishes on their heads. In them they carried their digging sticks, wooden scoops, and pieces of bark or wood used to separate seeds from chaff. They also carried round stones used to grind seeds into a kind of flour.

The Aboriginals never made or saw wheels. They had no domesticated animals except for dingoes. They wove no cloth. Therefore, they wore no clothes. (But in the coldest southern regions they made cloaks of possum skins or shaped kangaroo skins.) Life was simple but very demanding.

The women did learn to weave bags out of long grasses. They slung these bags over their backs, securing them with headbands. They carried eggs and manme (vegetable food) they collected back to camp in these bags.

An Aboriginal working on a wood carving

THE ABORIGINAL CAMPSITE

To start a fire, sometimes Aboriginals rubbed two sticks or stones together. This made sparks for igniting a mound of dry grass. When possible, wood from small trees was used for fuel.

Camps were pitched near water holes. Temporary housing was built to suit the weather or the season. In the cold, dry winters large sheets of bark were fashioned into A-frame tents. In the wet season beehive-shaped huts called wurleys were formed from tree branches. The branches were bent in the shape of igloos. These frames were covered with bark and grass.

Insects were always a problem. Smoky fires were built inside the wurleys to drive away the sand flies and mosquitoes.

A SPECIAL RACE?

In 1688 and 1699 an English buccaneer, William Dampier, visited the northwest and northeast coasts of what then was called New Holland. He described the Aboriginals as "the miserablest people on earth."

Many scientists believe that these Stone Age people belong to a separate race, the Australoids. Others think they are Caucasians. Their dark hair is neither straight nor kinky, but wavy. Young children often have blond hair. Some tribes are quite fair skinned, while others are dark skinned.

Clans were a family group associated by a myth, a totem, or by land. (A totem is an object used as an emblem.) Totems were usually a plant, animal, or rock and were sacred. They were thought to guard and guide a family or clan.

The elders of a clan made certain that the laws and taboos of the tribe were observed. Even today when someone is ill the Aboriginals might call a medicine man as well as a doctor from a nearby town or settlement.

TODAY'S ABORIGINALS

For thousands of years the Aboriginals roamed within their own tribal areas. With the arrival of the British settlers, however, their lands, especially along the eastern coast, were occupied by the newcomers.

However, the past decade has seen an enormous impetus for land rights by Aboriginal Australians. The government has recognized this. Aboriginals and Torres Strait islanders, representing 1.2 percent of the population, now hold title to 9.6

In the outback some Aboriginals work on cattle or sheep stations.

percent of the land area. They hold more than 282,000 square miles (730,000 square kilometers)—more than half of it inalienable freehold. This is an area about as large as East and West Germany and the United Kingdom combined. The land is rich in minerals, including bauxite, uranium, and natural gas.

The Federal Department of Aboriginal Affairs and state authorities work to promote education, to assist in forming policies, and to develop programs of benefit to Aboriginals.

In the 1976 Australian census, 160,000 people described themselves as Aboriginals. The number of Aboriginals declined dramatically as a result of European settlement, but their population has been increasing in recent years.

In the outback Aboriginals find jobs on cattle and sheep stations. Others work in special enterprises on Aboriginal land. In the cities they work in government and industry.

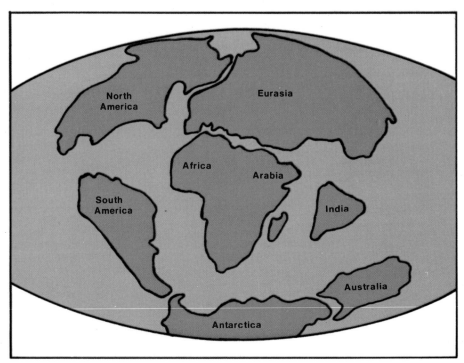

Scientists believe that about 200 million years ago, two landmasses,
Gondwanaland and Laurasia, existed (below). About 65 million years ago, the
earth looked like the map above. The continents as they exist today
were formed through millions of years of drifting landmasses.

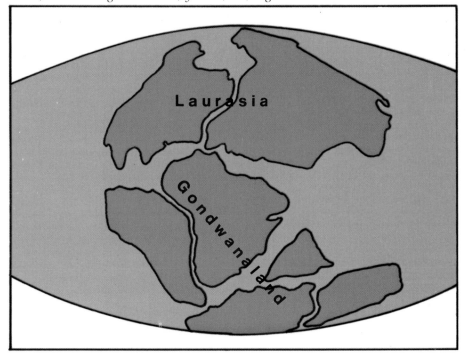

Chapter 3

A LAND OF

MANY HUES

Australia is probably the oldest of earth's landmasses. How it was formed geologists do not know for certain. There are several theories about its origin.

HOW IT BEGAN

Some geologists believe the continent rose out of the sea millions of years ago. They have found fossils that indicate the lowlands once were part of an ocean floor.

Others believe there was once a world continent that broke apart to form all of the continents and islands. Still others suggest there was the supercontinent called Gondwanaland. They say the continents of Africa, South America, Australia, and Antarctica and the islands of New Zealand and the subcontinent of India can be fit together like a jigsaw puzzle. This would form Gondwanaland. Each of these theories leaves many unanswered questions.

Scientists believe the Australian continent is older than Europe and North America. There are no high mountains as in the other continents. Whatever mountains did exist have been worn down. Even the Great Dividing Range is very low compared with the Alps or the Rockies or the Andes. The Great Dividing Range extends along the eastern edge of the continent.

The average altitude of these mountains is less than 3,000 feet (914 meters) in the northern and central sections. Several peaks in southeastern New South Wales are 1 mile (1,609 meters) in altitude. Mount Kosciusko in the Snowy Mountains of the Range is the highest peak, 7,310 feet (2,228 meters).

WHERE IS "DOWN UNDER"?

Geologists believe that for at least fifty million years the island continent has been isolated from other landmasses. There once may have been some land bridges to islands to the north and even to New Zealand. No one knows for sure.

Australia is more than twice as large as India. It is almost as large as the continental United States.

Sydney, the largest and oldest city, is as far south of the Equator as Los Angeles, California is north of it. Hobart, the capital of the southern island state of Tasmania, is as far south as Florence, Italy or Chicago, Illinois is north of the Equator.

The Arafura Sea separates Australia's northern coast from New Guinea. The Torres Strait separates Cape York Peninsula from Papua New Guinea. The Coral Sea, South Pacific Ocean, and Tasman Sea wash the eastern shores. Along the southern coast, the Pacific and Indian oceans become the southern ocean in the Great Australian Bight. The Timor Sea lies between the continent and Timor Island of Indonesia.

REEFS, HIGHLANDS, PLATEAUS, AND DESERTS

Australia can be divided in many ways. There are the political divisions: the six states of New South Wales, Victoria, South

*The Macdonnell Mountain Ranges
in the Northern Territory*

Australia, Western Australia, Queensland, and Tasmania. There is
also the Northern Territory, which has not yet been granted
statehood. Canberra, which is self-governing, is the main part of
the Australian Capital Territory. In addition, there are the
territorial islands and the Australian Antarctic Territory.

Australia might also be divided into three geographical sections:
the Eastern Highlands, the Eastern Lowlands, and the Western
Plateau.

A third division might be made according to vegetation. There
are small areas of dense rain forests where the rainfall is more
than 60 inches (152 centimeters) yearly. Forests, usually of
eucalyptus trees, are found mainly where rainfall averages
between 40 and 60 inches (101.6 and 152 centimeters). The
savannas have bushy shrubs. The shrubland in the southwest arid
region is called mallee, the name of dwarf eucalyptus. Where it is
even drier, grasses grow. In the driest desert area, the only time
vegetation appears is after a very rare rain. A desert with gravel or
loose stones is known as a gibber. It is a very barren, dry region.

Sections of the northern coast receive the heaviest rainfall.
Sections along the eastern coast also receive heavy rains, more
than 60 inches (152 centimeters) in some areas. Tasmania, too, has
very heavy rainfall over almost half of the island.

The eastern coast is humid. Moisture-laden winds blow in from the Pacific Ocean. The Great Dividing Range acts as a barrier that prevents much of the rain from moving farther inland. The rain falls on the fertile Eastern Highlands.

The western slopes of the highlands receive enough rain for farms and grazing properties. Farmers raise and harvest wheat and other grains. Cattle and sheep stations are smaller than those farther west where it takes several acres to feed a single animal.

The state of South Australia receives less rainfall than any other. Most of that state (87 percent) receives less than 12 inches (30.4 centimeters) a year. Almost half of Western Australia has less than 8 inches (20 centimeters) a year. One third of the country is desert or semidesert.

THE FACE OF THE LAND

The mountains were formed by volcanic eruptions. They were lifted up by the folding and faulting of the earth's crust. The landforms of the very dry region to the west resulted from erosion by wind and water. Seasonal monsoon rains may deluge the northernmost area in the summer. The heavy rains cause floods that wash away the barren soil.

Dry lakes and riverbeds, sand dunes and hills are found in the Western Plateau's red center. The most important of these formations is Ayers Rock. It is 1,143 feet (348 meters) high. Its base measures 5.5 miles (8.8 kilometers) in circumference. Nearby are the strange Olga Mountains. They consist of thirty red peaks that rise as much as 1,500 feet (457 meters). The peaks are separated by deep ravines. This area was sacred to the Aboriginals. Paintings in Ayers Rock caves illustrate Dreamtime.

Ayers Rock is a popular tourist spot.

Farther southwest in Western Australia are forests of eucalyptus trees. Abundant wild flowers bloom from September to April. Northward along the Indian Ocean the land becomes semidesert.

Tasmania is an island state 150 miles (241 kilometers) off the southeast coast of the mainland. It has some of the country's most beautiful scenery. An extension of the Australian Alps is snow-covered in winter. In summer visitors flock to this southernmost state. They hike on trails in its national parks and reserves.

Australia's island territories include Norfolk Island, which is of volcanic origin. It is approximately 1,000 miles (1,609 kilometers) east-northeast of Sydney. The island is only 5 miles (8 kilometers) long and 2.5 miles (4 kilometers) wide. Pineapples, citrus fruits, and vegetables are grown. Tourists vacation on its beaches.

More than 340 species of coral grow in the Great Barrier Reef.

Australia has claimed one fourth of Antarctica. Six other nations also claim parts. Australia has three permanent research stations on frozen Antarctica. A fourth station is on Macquarie Island between Tasmania and Antarctica.

The Great Barrier Reef is one of nature's most fascinating wonders. It stretches for more than 1,200 miles (1,931 kilometers) along the northern half of the east coast of Australia from Gladstone to Cape York. Hundreds of coral reefs and colorful islands attract visitors. The waters have hundreds of species of brilliantly colored fish. More than 340 species of coral grow in many shapes and colors. Beautiful birds live on the islands.

There are contrasts in color and hue throughout the country. There are lush green tropical rain forests and the red soils of the gibber desert. There are wintry white mountains and sandy-colored western plateaus. Farms, cities, cattle and sheep stations, and the lonely outback add to the many hues of an ancient land and a young nation.

Chapter 4
"DISCOVERED" AT LAST

For fourteen hundred years Europeans believed in the existence of *Terra Australis Incognita,* the Unknown Southern Land. They had no knowledge that the Aboriginals had reached the southern continent forty thousand years before. The Aboriginals had no written language with which to communicate their discovery. They had no means to return to the region from which they had traveled. It is possible that Indonesian sailors discovered the continent. If they did, they failed to report their discovery.

Luis Vaez de Torres, a Spanish captain, sailed from Peru in December, 1605. His ship was carried southwest by monsoon winds. Months later he sailed near the Great Barrier Reef. Torres traveled north and then west through the strait that is named for him. He skirted the shores of New Guinea. There is no record, however, that he sighted *Terra Australis.*

That same year Dutch explorers in the *Duyfken* (Little Dove) under Captain Willem Jansz reached the west coast of what is now Cape York Peninsula, landing at Albatross Bay. In the books of the Dutch East India Company it was recorded, "No good to be done there." The land was desolate.

Between 1616 and 1627 six Dutch expeditions sailed along the northern western, and southern shores. They named the continent New Holland.

This pewter plate, in the National Library in Canberra, carries an inscription recording two Dutch landings in Western Australia, one in 1616 and the other in 1697.

Dutch mariner Abel Tasman sighted what he thought was the southern extension of New Holland in November, 1642. He did not know it was an island.

The Dutch found nothing of value in this land. But they did not want other countries exploring New Holland. Such exploration might hurt their rich trade in Dutch Indonesia. So they spread word that the land was worthless.

The British ship *Cygnet* reached the west coast of New Holland in January, 1688. William Dampier was aboard. Later he wrote a book, *New Voyage Around the World.* He stated, "I am certain it joins neither Asia, Africa, or America."

Dampier returned in 1699. The Aboriginals were unfriendly. He was unable to find fresh water. Disappointed, he returned to England. He said the land was not suited for settlement.

CAPTAIN COOK REACHES THE UNKNOWN LAND

A British expedition led by James Cook sailed from England in 1768. In Tahiti, Cook and his scientists were to watch the planet Venus passing between the sun and Earth. But Cook had secret instructions to sail farther in search of *Terra Australis.*

On board Cook's ship, the *Endeavour,* were Charles Green, an astronomer; Joseph Banks, a naturalist; Dr. Carl Solander, a Swedish botanist; and two artists who were to identify and paint the scenery, plants, and animals of Tahiti.

Cook sailed westward from Tahiti. He mapped many of the islands he discovered and claimed them for Great Britain. Weeks later one of the seamen sighted land. It was the east coast of New Zealand. Cook charted the coastline as he sailed around the two islands. Then strong southerly gales drove the ship northward. The *Endeavour* reached the southeast coast of New Holland. No earlier expedition had sighted this coast. The terrain was very different from what the others had seen.

Nine days after Lieutenant Hicks sighted land in April, 1770, the men went ashore farther north. The area was later named Botany Bay for its rich plant life. Carefully the two artists recorded the unusual plant life Banks and Solander found.

The bay teemed with fish. Fresh water was available. But Cook was concerned that there were no fresh fruits or vegetables. There also were no animals for meat. They did see Aboriginals.

On May 7, the *Endeavour* set sail for the north. It passed the entrance to a harbor Cook called Port Jackson. Sydney is now located on that harbor. Much farther north the ship was grounded and damaged on a coral reef. Cook managed to get the ship to a bay a short distance north. The sailors repaired the damaged hull.

--- Captain Cook's 1770 trip

A portrait of Captain James Cook

Meanwhile, the scientists and artists explored ashore. They found kangaroos, wallabies, crocodiles, turtles, and dingoes. There were many tropical birds to describe and sketch. And there were Aboriginals who came to their camp. The men were fascinated.

The ship continued north. It reached the tip of the continent that Cook named Cape York. He made no claims to the land to the west. He wrote, "The east coast I am confident was never seen or visited by any Europeans before us."

Cook hoisted the British flag and took possession in the name of King George III. He named the cape for the king's brother. He named the eastern coast of the continent New South Wales.

An artist's conception of the first settlement

By 1776 England was involved in a war with the American colonists. English jails were overcrowded. It was impossible to continue to send convicts to the American colonies. But judges continued to sentence convicted persons to life outside their own country. Where could they be sent?

Joseph Banks offered a solution. Send the convicts to New South Wales. Botany Bay, Banks suggested, would be an ideal place for them. Some of these people had been convicted of breaking very minor laws.

On May 13, 1787, the First Fleet set sail for New South Wales. There were eleven ships under the command of Captain Arthur Phillip. Of the 1,138 persons aboard, 821 were convicts.

At the Cape of Good Hope in southern Africa, Captain Phillip stopped for supplies. He had brought grain from England but he added to the supply. He also purchased horses, cows and bulls, sheep, and pigs. He selected plants and trees for the new colony— bananas, oranges, lemons, apples, pears, figs, bamboo, oaks, and myrtle. The new colony was to establish itself as soon as possible.

An Australian stamp commemorates Matthew Flinders's circumnavigation of the continent.

Eight months after leaving England, Captain Phillip brought his ships into Botany Bay. They had traveled 15,000 miles (24,135 kilometers). Phillip soon discovered Botany Bay was not the best place to settle. So the fleet moved north. They entered the bay Captain Cook had passed and called Port Jackson. Phillip described it as "the finest harbor in the world in which a thousand sails may ride in the most perfect security."

On January 26, 1788, Phillip landed in what he called Sydney Cove. He raised the Union Jack and fired shots in honor of the new settlement. January 26 is now celebrated as Australia Day, a national holiday.

In 1802–1803 Matthew Flinders circumnavigated the continent. He mapped the entire coast. He was the first to note the extent of the continent. He suggested it be called "Australia."

By then the eastern half of the continent was claimed by Great Britain. In 1817 the governor of New South Wales used the name "Australia" officially for the first time. In 1829 the western half was claimed. The entire continent then was under British rule.

The convicts who lived in the settlement at Port Arthur in Van Diemen's Land (now Tasmania) had a harsh life and were cut off from the rest of the colony. The ruins of the settlement are now preserved.

THE FIRST COLONY

The first convict colony at Sydney Cove faced many hardships. For six months the people lived in tents. Finally huts were built. The frames were timbers and the walls panels of cabbage-tree trunks. The eucalyptus (red gum) wood was too hard. The tools the men had brought could not cut them down. They could not saw them into lumber. Besides, there were few men with skills in construction work.

The little colony faced starvation the first two years. Captain Phillip waited for the first supply ship. He did not know it had been wrecked on an iceberg. Finally, the *Lady Juliana* arrived in June, 1789. It brought more convicts and few supplies.

The next ship, the *Justinian*, brought John Macarthur, an officer of the regiment assigned to the colony. Macarthur secured a grant of land west of Sydney. Here he grazed a few sheep. Later he discovered sixty-one cattle near the colony. The tiny herd Phillip had brought in 1788 had wandered away. The herd had increased. Macarthur decided the cattle must have been smart enough to pick a good grazing area. He selected land there. He began Australia's famous merino wool industry on that land.

AN EXPANDING POPULATION

Most of the early immigrants came unwillingly. For fifty years 90 percent of the settlers were convicts. In 1840 convict immigration to New South Wales ended. In Van Diemen's Land, now Tasmania, such immigration ended in 1852. In Western Australia, however, the free colony requested convicts from 1850 to 1868. The convicts helped clear land, build roads, and construct housing. A total of 162,000 convicts were sent to Australia.

The Blue Mountains of the Great Dividing Range were a barrier for early settlers. Only the coastal regions were inhabited. More grazing land was needed for the increasing number of sheep and cattle. Finally in 1813 three men found a ridge route. It led them to the Western Plateau. Later that year G.W. Evans, a surveyor, crossed the mountains. He found the fertile, well-watered land good for grazing and raising wheat. Governor Macquarie ordered a road built across the mountains. It was completed in 1815. The first inland town, Bathurst, was founded.

Other towns were started along the coast: Brisbane in 1824, Perth in 1829, Melbourne in 1835, and Adelaide in 1836. Hobart, Tasmania, was settled on its present site in 1804.

A whaling captain's house, built in 1810, has been restored in Liverpool, west of Sydney.

By 1792 some trade with the outside world had begun. Ships arrived from England, India, China, and the United States. Captain Phillip was appointed governor of New South Wales when the First Fleet landed. When he sailed for England in December, 1792, the community in Australia was struggling. Although small farms and gardens produced some fruits and vegetables, nourishing food was scarce. Life in Australia was a constant battle for survival.

DEVELOPING AN ECONOMY

On his circumnavigation Matthew Flinders landed on what he called Kangaroo Island. He found seals as well as kangaroos. Sealers and whalers soon were busy in Australian waters. They used Sydney Cove as a base.

In 1791 five English whaling ships had arrived with convicts and supplies for Sydney. The first American whaler anchored in the harbor in 1802. Whale oil was in great demand. Sealers also were busy. Sealskins brought a good price in China, England, and the United States. Between 1800 and 1806, 14,750 sealskins were exported, together with 2,756 tons (2,500 metric tonnes) of sperm-whale oil.

An elephant seal

Whaling stations were built along the coast. Bull sperm whales often measured 70 feet (21 meters). Their blubber, when melted down, produced a fatty oil for use in oil lamps. The meat was sold to the settlers. Other by-products also were salable.

Fur seals were taken for their skins. They also yielded oil. Elephant seals also were captured for their oil. The ruins of an old sealing station can be found on Macquarie Island. An Australian sealer discovered fur and elephant seals on Macquarie in 1810. Fur sealing on Macquarie ended in 1919.

The last whaling station on the continent was closed in November, 1978. It was located at Albany, Western Australia. It began operations in the 1840s. Australia banned whaling in its waters in 1979. By January 1981 it also had banned the import of all whale products.

A flock of sheep near Cowra, New South Wales

WOOL ENTERS THE ECONOMY

The production of wool became important to the country's economy. Like sealskins and sperm oil, wool was easily transported. In 1801 John Macarthur sailed for England. He returned to the colony in 1805 knowing that English woolen mills would gladly buy all the wool the colony could produce.

Sheep raising became successful. Australia is still the world's major producer and exporter of wool. At a rough estimate, about 14 percent—135 million head—of the world's sheep are here.

Cattle, too, soon became important. In 1796 there were a few hundred cattle on small farms. Many more roamed in unfenced areas, descendants of those on the First Fleet.

As new areas opened up, dairying became important. Beef cattle increased in number. Australian "mobs," as herds are called, total roughly 26 million head of cattle.

RAISING CROPS

By 1790 the settlers had planted wheat, barley, and maize. Today wheat is a major crop wherever there is enough moisture.

Irrigation, crop rotation, the use of fertilizers and trace elements, and soil conservation increase crop yield. Crops can be planted on new land using these measures.

Australia has the world's largest artesian basin. Water is held deep underground. It is brought to the surface by wells or bores.

A NATION IS BORN

New South Wales gained more and more administrative power as time passed. The distance between Great Britain and the Australian continent was great. Communication was slow. Other colonies of the continent wanted their own governments instead of being governed through New South Wales. The British passed the Australian Colonies Act of 1850. This act allowed the colonies to draft their own constitutions.

GOLD!

In 1851 gold was discovered. Immigrants from many countries poured in. The value of the gold exported to Great Britain between 1852 and 1870 was greater than the value of wool shipped there.

WORKING FOR A FEDERAL GOVERNMENT

A federal government was needed. Meetings were held beginning in 1863. Finally in 1891 an Australian constitution was

The Parliament House in Canberra, where the government has met since 1927

drafted. Ten years later, the Commonwealth of Australia was founded. On January 1, 1901, the six former colonies became states. The new nation was a reality. The Northern Territory is expected to attain statehood in the near future.

At first the parliament met in Melbourne. Then a federal capital territory was selected.

CANBERRA AND THE AUSTRALIAN CAPITAL TERRITORY

New South Wales gave the land for the new capital city, Canberra. *Canberra* is an Aboriginal word. It means "meeting place." An international competition was held to provide a city plan. Walter Burley Griffin, an American architect from Chicago, was the winner.

Beautiful government buildings surround a lake. Some are the National Library, Parliament House, the High Court, and the National Gallery. Nearby are the Academy of Sciences and the National War Memorial.

The National Library of Australia, in Canberra, has over three million volumes.

Canberra is on the western slopes of the Great Dividing Range. Visitors can look down on the city from Mount Ainslie.

About one quarter of a million people live in the Australian Capital Territory.

GOVERNING THE COMMONWEALTH

Parliament has two bodies, the House of Representatives and the Senate. The House has 125 members. The Senate has ten members from each of the six states and two each from the Northern Territory and the Australian Capital Territory. Senators are elected for six years and representatives for three years. The prime minister is the leader of the political party with a majority in the House of Representatives.

Queen Elizabeth II is represented by a governor-general and six state governors. The governor-general exercises power through the Federal Executive Council. The prime minister and the cabinet direct the departments of the government. The number of ministers in the cabinet varies. In 1983 Labor government began office with twenty-six ministers.

Australians were the first people to vote by secret ballot. Voting is a legal duty. Everyone eighteen years of age and older must vote in all elections. Persons who do not vote can be fined.

Australia is a democracy. It is an independent nation with a federal constitution. It is a member of the British Commonwealth of Nations. It is also a member of the United Nations.

Chapter 5

ANIMALS AND PLANTS FROM OUT OF THE PAST

The Australian coat of arms pictures the kangaroo, emu, and wattle. No other country can claim these three as its own. Man's history on Australia began about forty thousand years ago. But animals must have lived there for seventy-five million years. No other area of the world has so many animals that are so unusual. Of the native mammals, there are no hoofed animals—deer or horses. There are no members of the cat family—lions, panthers, or leopards. There are no primates—monkeys or apes.

About half of the 230 species of mammals in Australia are marsupials. A marsupial female has a pouch. Newborn baby animals climb into the pouch to feed on their mother's milk. They stay inside until they are old enough to find their own food.

WHERE THE ROO AND THE WALLABY ROAM

We saw "an animal something less than a greyhound, of a mouse color, very slender made and swift of foot," wrote Joseph Banks, the naturalist with Cook, in 1770. Cook himself tried to describe these animals to Englishmen. He was greeted with laughter. Who had ever heard of a creature like the kangaroo?

A wombat is a marsupial. The mother carries her young in a pouch until they develop.

The red and gray kangaroos are the largest marsupials. The smallest are no larger than a mouse. Some marsupials live in trees. Some with kitelike membranes sail through the air from tree to tree. Some, such as the wombat, have backward-opening pouches and dig burrows. Some, such as the red kangaroo and the wallaby, graze in the central grasslands. Others, such as the gray kangaroo, graze in the low scrub and forests. There are forty-five species of "roos," as the Australians call them.

How surprised the early settlers must have been when they saw their first kangaroos. Gray kangaroos are 7 feet tall (2.1 meters) when they sit upright. They rest on their 10-inch-long (254-millimeter) feet, supported by their strong tails. At rest, they hold their short forelegs in front.

When they are about eight months old, the little "joeys" poke their heads out of their mothers' pouches. Soon they leave the pouches to feed by themselves. But they dash back to mother at the first alarm. They dive headfirst into the pouches and squirm around to look out.

Koalas eat the leaves of the eucalyptus tree.

THE KOALA

The koala is a marsupial. Many people call these animals koala bears. Even though their scientific name means "pouched bear," they are not true bears.

Unlike the kangaroo, the koala mother's pouch opens to the rear. Koalas feed on the leaves of certain eucalyptus trees. Some people think a substance in the leaves makes them permanently drowsy. *Koala* is an Aboriginal name. It means "no drink." Koalas very rarely drink water. They are nocturnal animals. They sleep during the day in eucalyptus trees.

Adult koalas are about 2 feet (.6 meters) high with gray brown fur. They have large furry ears and a leathery-looking nose. Baby koalas spend six months in their mother's pouch. Then they climb out and cling to the mother's back. They are quite helpless until they are a year old.

Above: The platypus can only be found in Australia.
Below: The echidna, or spiny anteater, eats ants and termites.

Their pelts are so soft that millions of koalas were killed half a century ago. The animals almost became extinct. Now government protection is enforced. The koala has only one baby every two years. It is taking a long time to increase the population.

TWO OF THE WORLD'S MOST PRIMITIVE

The most primitive and most strange of all Australian animals are the monotremes. The platypus and the spiny anteater are egg-laying mammals.

"That animal was put together by a committee," said a visitor watching a platypus at Sydney's Taronga Park Zoo. The platypus spends only a few hours in the water each day. Like all mammals it must come up for air. Visitors see an animal with a furry coat, a ducklike bill, and webbed feet like an otter's. The flat tail is like a beaver's. The male has a poison fang or spur on each hind foot.

The female platypus usually lays two eggs. She wraps herself around them to incubate them deep in a burrow she has dug in a riverbank.

The young hatch in about ten days. They begin to feed on milk that breaks out like sweat on the mother's abdomen. Seventeen weeks later they will forage on the muddy bottoms of freshwater streams or lakes for crayfish and small fish.

The spiny anteater rarely is seen. It has a long snout and sticky tongue to catch ants and termites. The female lays eggs. When the young hatch they crawl into a pouch which females develop only during the breeding season.

All of the country's animals have learned to adapt to conditions that range from arid to tropical. They have survived throughout millions of years. They are unique.

WITH AND WITHOUT WINGS

The Australian bird life is unique, too. There are about 750 known species on the continent. There are about 600 resident (non-migratory) species. Of these, 383 species are unique to Australia. There are no woodpeckers, vultures, or flamingos. However, there are 60 different species of parrots. Birds such as petrels and albatross stop over on migrations north or south.

Royal, King, Gentoo, and Rockhopper penguins breed on Macquarie Island. The Fairy or Little Blue penguins can be found in burrows on Phillip Island near Melbourne.

Some birds are related to species found elsewhere. The black swan, Cape Barren goose, and magpie goose are three of these.

The lyrebird is found only in Australia. It has 2-foot-long (61-centimeter) tail feathers. The male spreads out its tail while it sings and dances to attract a female. Once the breeding season is over, the male loses his tail plumes. For ten weeks he is drab and quiet, scratching for worms. The lyrebird rarely flies.

The emu, a flightless bird, is found throughout mainland Australia. The ostrich, which the emu resembles, is the only larger bird. Emus reach a height of 6 feet (1.8 meters) and may weigh 130 pounds (59 kilograms). They have undeveloped wings hidden under dull brown, coarse, hairlike feathers.

After the female has laid 7 to 11 dark gray green eggs, the male takes over. He incubates the eggs for eight weeks. After they hatch he continues to take care of the chicks.

Adult emus can take giant strides. They can run at speeds of more than 30 miles (50 kilometers) an hour when attacked. They are curious birds who live on roots, fruits, leaves, and grass.

Australia has about
750 species of birds.
Above: Emus are large
flightless birds.
Left: Gentoo penguins
breed on Macquarie
Island. Bottom right:
A young girl is visited
by parrots in an open-air market.

The kookaburra is a member of the kingfisher family.

The cassowary is a cousin of the ostrich. Cassowaries are more colorful than emus. Their spiny hard feathers are dark blue black. Their necks are blue and red. They live in tropical rain forests, eating fruits and berries. They have powerful legs so they can run as fast as emus. The helmetlike crests on their heads protect them when they crash through brush and vines.

The kookaburra has forgotten how to fish. But it is a member of the kingfisher family. Instead, kookaburras feed on insects, mice, and small snakes. Farmers like kookaburras despite their loud, cackling, laughing sounds. The "laughing jackass" has a diet helpful to farmers.

Australia has about seven hundred species of acacia, many with brightly colored flowers.

THE COLDBLOODED VERTEBRATES

Australia has a large number of lizards, snakes, turtles, and tortoises. There are also two species of crocodiles. In addition, there are many kinds of frogs and toads.

Many of Australia's fish, insects, and spiders are found nowhere else. This is especially true of the nine hundred species of ants.

ACACIA AND EUCALYPTUS

The settlers looked for native materials for constructing their houses. They found acacias especially good for weaving into fences, roofs, and the framework for mud-plastered walls. They used the term "wattling" instead of "weaving." Before long the acacia became known as the wattle. Its usefulness and beautiful blossoms earned it a place on the nation's coat of arms. Of the world's 930 species of acacias, three fourths grow here.

Eucalyptus trees are found throughout Australia.

There are about 450 distinct forms of eucalyptus trees, plus many natural and artificial hybrids. These hardwoods provide lumber and material for paper and newsprint. Oil distilled from the leaves is used in medicine. They can be found where the rainfall is less than 10 inches (254 millimeters), as well as in the tropical regions. Some species, such as the mountain ash of Tasmania and Victoria, are the tallest hardwoods in the world. Stunted eucalyptus can be found in the outback.

Flowers of the silk oak tree

FANTASTIC FLOWERS

Western Australia is called the wild flower state. At least two thousand species of small flowering plants grow along the western coastal regions and the southwest corner of the continent. The state flower of Western Australia is the kangaroo paw. This woolly flower resembles the paw of a kangaroo. Wild flowers can be found throughout the country.

Jungles of tree ferns grow in some areas. Low-growing ferns abound in the bush. In the tropical rain forests, orchids add color to the land.

The wheel and some wood of an old cart left to rot in the dry country

THE DRY OUTBACK

There are few creeks and rivers in the desert and semiarid outback. Trees and shrubs must send their roots deep into the soil to seek water. In September, during a short springtime, rains may come. Emus and kangaroos delight in the quick-growing vegetation. Then, in a few weeks, the land is dry again. The sun beats down mercilessly. The creeks and rivers dry up. Birds and animals must search for food and water.

PROTECTING NATIVE PLANTS AND ANIMALS

Some of Australia's unique mammals have become extinct. Cattle and sheep have packed down the once soft soil. Burrowing animals such as the marsupial mouse and the kangaroo rat cannot dig down for shelter from the merciless heat. They cannot survive.

For many years the owners and managers of the stations killed kangaroos to stop them from grazing. They wanted the grasses for their own animals. Government regulations now protect the kangaroos. Today's kangaroo population is estimated at thirty-two million.

Australia has strict laws protecting all its native animals. In most cases the animals are increasing in number. The National Parks and Wildlife Service was established to protect, manage, and control wildlife. State and national parks have been set aside in the interest of wildlife conservation.

Chapter 6
A LAND OF CONTRASTS

There are vast contrasts in climate, temperature, resources, and scenery throughout the continent, the islands, and the internal territories. Australia is a land rich in many natural resources. But in many regions there is little of man's most important resource, water.

Two thirds of the people live in the coastal state capitals. In the two thirds of the country that is desert or semidesert, population is sparse.

To develop its industry, resources, and economic strength, Australia needed more people. The country has welcomed immigrants. They have come from a hundred different countries since World War II. New immigrants now number well over one hundred thousand a year.

Immigrants are helped to settle where their skills can contribute most to Australia's developing economy. All six states have acquired new settlers, including refugees from countries such as Vietnam. They all find a country of great diversity, with many nationalities represented among its citizens.

The southern coast of New South Wales

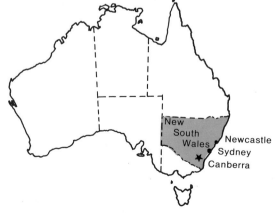

NEW SOUTH WALES—THE OLDEST COLONY

Captain Cook gave the name New South Wales to the eastern half of the continent. Other colonies were formed from New South Wales. Finally it was left with 10 percent of Australia's land area. It is fourth in size but has about 35 percent of the country's population.

Sydney is Australia's largest port and the capital of New South Wales. On either side of the harbor there are bays and inlets rimmed with red-tiled-roof houses. Beautiful beaches provide recreation north and south of the harbor. The city's residents enjoy 340 days of sunshine each year.

Thousands of people live across the harbor from the main business and shopping section. They take commuter ferries to work each day. On some routes hydrofoils skim over the water.

A favorite ferry route crosses to Taronga Park Zoo. The zoo has a collection of Australian animals—koalas, kangaroos, wallabies, emus, and platypuses. It is built on the side of a ridge. *Taronga* is the Aboriginal word for "water view."

Sydney Harbor Bridge connects the city proper with the north shore. Rising high above the water, it is an impressive single-span steel arch bridge.

The most striking building in the whole country is Sydney Opera House. It was completed in 1973 on Bennelong Point. Its unusual roof was designed to look like sails in the harbor.

Skyscrapers rise in the business section. Australia Tower has a restaurant on the fiftieth floor. Visitors have a complete view of Sydney and surrounding suburbs and beaches.

Manly, a suburb of Sydney, is located at the entrance to Port Jackson. It is a short ferry ride to Manly from the Sydney

Above: The Botanical Gardens in Sydney
Below: The bridge that spans Sydney Harbor was opened in 1932.

Above: The Sydney Opera House with its saillike roofs opened in 1973. Below: Skyscrapers and expressways of modern Sydney

Manly Beach is in a suburb of Sydney. Governor Phillip named this area Manly in 1788 when he saw the manly bearing of the natives.

commuter docks. There are sixteen beaches on the ocean and harbor. The suburb also has an interesting aquarium with exhibits of sharks and fish from Australian waters.

North of Sydney on the Hawkesbury River a ferry carries mail, supplies, and passengers to homes where the river is the only "road" for the residents. The scenery is beautiful with lovely inlets and high cliffs.

There is more to New South Wales than Sydney and its suburbs. It raises over 33 percent of the nation's wheat, more than 90 percent of the rice, almost 75 percent of the cotton, 24 percent of the beef cattle, and more than 17 percent of the cattle for milk production. It also produces one third of the country's wool. Other crops are raised in the well-watered coastal zone.

Newcastle is located 100 miles (161 kilometers) north of Sydney. Coal mines in the area are important to the giant steel mills in the city. Wollongong, south of Sydney, also has coal resources and steel mills.

Parkes is 250 miles (402 kilometers) west of Sydney over the Great Dividing Range. It is the center of the great wheat-growing and sheep-grazing western plains of the state. Nearby is a huge radio telescope. It picked up and transmitted pictures of America's Apollo astronauts on the moon. It also measures the energy from the sun and distant stars. Visitors are welcome at Parkes' National Radio Astronomy Observatory.

This telescope is run by the C.S.I.R.O., the Commonwealth Scientific and Industrial Research Organization. Scientists in the C.S.I.R.O. work in five institutes. They have forty research divisions throughout the country. Their studies have benefited science and industry.

TASMANIA—THE SMALLEST STATE

Tasmania is Australia's smallest state. It has less than 1 percent of the country's land area. It is separated from the continent by Bass Strait, 150 miles (241 kilometers) wide. The island was called Van Diemen's Land until 1855.

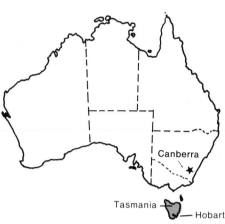

The Tasman Bridge crosses the Derwent River at Hobart, Tasmania.

Captain Cook landed on the island in 1777. But it was not until 1802 that it was claimed by Great Britain. Hobart was the first permanent settlement, founded on its new site in 1804. In 1825 Tasmania became a separate colony. Hobart served as a penal colony until 1852.

Hobart's harbor is one of the finest in the world. It is especially busy from February to May when the apple and pear crops are shipped. Tasmania is known as the Apple Isle. Orchards are found near Hobart. A jam factory, cocoa and chocolate factory, fabric plant, zinc smelter, and many other industries make Hobart an important industrial city.

Launceston is 40 miles (64 kilometers) from Bass Strait on the Tamar River. It was never a penal colony. Its busy port handles fruit, wool, textiles, and timber. There are large wool-spinning and textile mills.

Tasmania is mountainous and heavily forested. The island has beautiful scenery. Tourists and residents find its national parks inviting for bushwalking. Alpine flowers, two hundred species of birds, and lush forests attract an ever increasing number of tourists. Snowcapped mountains in winter, rushing streams, and tumbling waterfalls add to the island's beauty.

The rivers have been dammed. Water is piped down the mountainsides to hydroelectric plants that generate electricity. They provide power for an aluminum smelter in northern Tasmania.

WESTERN AUSTRALIA—THE FABULOUS WEST

Western Australia became the third colony in 1829. But it did not receive self-government from Great Britain until 1890. It is the country's largest state. Western Australia covers one third of the continent.

The first settlement was at Albany in 1826. The Aboriginals in the area were hostile. They had been mistreated by sealers who went ashore at the harbor first charted in 1791 by Captain George Vancouver.

In February, 1840, Edward Eyre set out on a 1,000-mile (1,609-kilometer) exploration westward from Adelaide. Following the coast, he traveled over the Nullarbor Plain (no trees plain). He found a flat limestone region 400 miles (644 kilometers) long almost without vegetation. Only a few small shrubs and wisps of

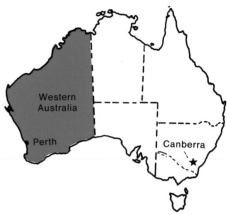

Perth is the capital of Western Australia.

grass grew on this extremely dry plateau. The Nullarbor Plain
stretches across both South Australia and Western Australia.
Eyre's journey was extremely difficult. He and an Aboriginal
named Wylie finally reached Albany in July, 1841.

In 1829, Captain Charles Fremantle sailed north after rounding
the southwestern cape of the continent. He took possession of the
land around the Swan River. Fremantle, at the mouth of the river,
is an important seaport and industrial city.

Ten miles (16 kilometers) up the Swan River, Perth was
established in 1829. It later became the capital of the colony and
state. Perth is far from the cities in the east. For years its only
contact was by sea until a telegraph line connected it with
Adelaide in 1877. Many years later a railway was built across the
state from Perth through Kalgoorlie and on to Sydney.

Gold was discovered in Coolgardie in 1892. The next year three prospectors found nuggets in the red sand of gullies at Kalgoorlie. Two hundred thousand people rushed into the area searching for gold. Water was so scarce that it cost several dollars a gallon. Kalgoorlie, 371 road miles (597 kilometers) from Perth, is on the western edge of the Nullarbor Plain and the Great Victoria Desert.

Irrigation is used to water large wheat fields 350 miles (563 kilometers) east of Perth. A pipeline from a reservoir near Perth carries water to Kalgoorlie. Irrigation near Norseman helps farmers grow oats, barley, and wheat. Stockmen raise "mobs" of sheep and cattle.

The Great Sandy, Gibson, and Great Victoria deserts cover much of the eastern section of the state. But southwest is wheat and wool country. There are lovely forests of karri and jarrah (eucalyptus) trees.

This, too, is the region of wild flowers. Stirling National Park is north of Albany. There one can find many of the 2,400 species of flora native only to southwest Australia.

King's Park is a large botanical garden in downtown Perth with many wild flowers.

SOUTH AUSTRALIA—DESERT AND OASIS

South Australia became the fourth separate colony in 1834. It was a free colony with no convicts.

Between 1828 and 1830 Captain Charles Sturt, a soldier in the British army, made two trips inland. His trips established the basic courses of the main rivers of eastern Australia.

In 1836 Lieutenant Colonel William Light selected a site on Gulf St. Vincent for a town. Adelaide became the capital of the colony

Adelaide is known as the City of Churches.

and is known as the City of Churches. It is also called the City of Culture. Every two years in March it celebrates a Festival of the Arts with music, drama, dance, and light entertainment. Its beautiful Festival Centre is a multipurpose complex overlooking the Torrens River and parkland.

The green belt of South Australia's coast slips away into semiarid land and desert 200 miles (322 kilometers) north. In August, 1844, Captain Sturt set out from Adelaide with fifteen men to explore this vast territory to the north. His expedition included horses, carts, bullocks, sheep, dogs, and a whaling boat to be assembled when Sturt reached a great inland sea he believed existed.

Adelaide's townspeople came out to cheer Sturt and his men on their way. The men pressed on across a stony desert now called a gibber, the most barren of all arid lands. Finally they reached a water hole. For six months they camped beside it. They named the place Fort Grey. The heat was unbearable. The temperature reached 130 degrees Fahrenheit (54.4 degrees Celsius) in the shade. It was so dry that nails fell out of the men's boots.

Sturt made the decision to press northward. They staggered on another 450 miles (724 kilometers). They had traveled 800 miles (1,287 kilometers) from Adelaide. At last they were forced to turn back. There had been no great inland sea. In January, 1846, the little party, minus one, returned to Adelaide. The red desert had taken its toll. Captain Sturt was blind and barely alive. Fortunately he recovered and continued to serve the government until 1853 when he returned to England.

Lake Eyre lies 450 miles (724 kilometers) north of Adelaide. It is 52 feet (16 meters) below sea level. Sturt had discovered Cooper Creek on his journey north. The creek and several small rivers

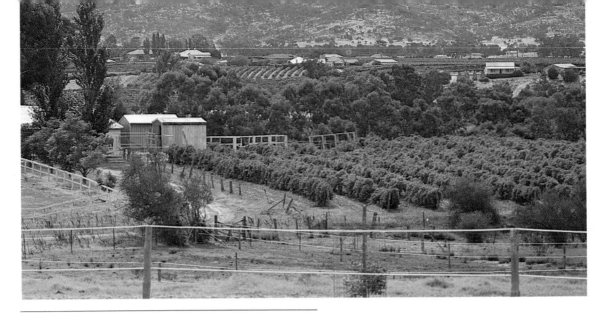

Wine will be made from the harvest of this vineyard.

feed into Lake Eyre. However, there is water in the lake only during the rainy season. During the dry months the water evaporates. The lake becomes a giant salt pan.

Aboriginal tribes still live in the outback on Aboriginal reserves. In November, 1981, the state gave the Pitjantjatjara people title to 40,000 square miles (103,600 square kilometers). This is one tenth of the area of the state. It was their traditional tribal land. The region has an opal field and large mineral resources. South Australia is the first state to grant such rights to Aboriginals. The federal government has provided land rights in its territories and negotiations are underway between the Aboriginals and governments of the other states. Mineral resources in the state include iron ore, coal, copper, zinc, and uranium. Deposits of limestone, essential in making steel, are found near the coast.

The fertile coastal belt has extensive vineyards. There are wheat fields and thousands of sheep. South Australia is a prosperous state. There are steel mills, oil refineries, and shipbuilding yards. Household appliance, automobile, and other factories have been established. Cargo is shipped from Port Adelaide.

VICTORIA—THE GARDEN STATE

Lieutenant Hicks on the *Endeavour* in 1770 was the first to sight the southeastern coast. The first permanent settlement in what eventually became the state of Victoria was established in 1835. When the population of the settlement reached five hundred in 1837, the town was named Melbourne. Since no convicts were sent to the area, the colonists asked to be separated from New South Wales. Their petition was granted in 1851. The many gardens in Melbourne and other towns have given the state its nickname, the Garden State.

Victoria is the smallest mainland state. It comprises only 3 percent of the country's total area. Its northern boundary with New South Wales is the Murray River.

In 1840 Count Paul Strzelecki led a party from Sydney over the rugged Snowy Mountains. He discovered Australia's highest peak, naming it Mount Kosciusko. Continuing south, the group crossed a fertile region in Victoria which Strzelecki called Gippsland in honor of Governor Gipps of New South Wales. The men finally reached Melbourne.

When gold was discovered in 1851, prospectors poured in. Many failed to strike it rich. They acquired land for farming or sheep and cattle raising.

Forests and national parks cover 30 percent of the state. Brown coal deposits provide fuel for generating stations. Oil refineries and petrochemical plants use crude oil from wells off the southeastern coast. Wheat, wool, butter, beef, plastics, and fresh and dried fruits are shipped from Melbourne and Geelong, the state's second largest city.

Melbourne is an important financial capital. Its major industrial

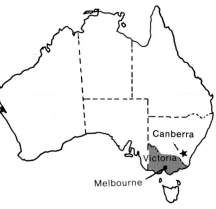

The business section of Melbourne is on the northern bank of the Yarra River.

products include automotive products, rubber products, agricultural machinery, textiles, clothing, and processed foods.

Pears, apples, and citrus fruits are boxed and shipped to other countries. Melbourne rivals Sydney as a commercial and industrial city.

Tourists enjoy visits to the Gippsland lakes, the ski country, and the Grampian Mountains with their wild flowers and birds. The penguin parade at Phillip Island also is popular. The little Fairy penguins swim ashore each night. Once on the beach, they stand upright and waddle toward their burrows in the tussock grass dunes. The manager of the penguin reserve then turns on a spotlight. Crowds watch the penguins, which are undisturbed by the light.

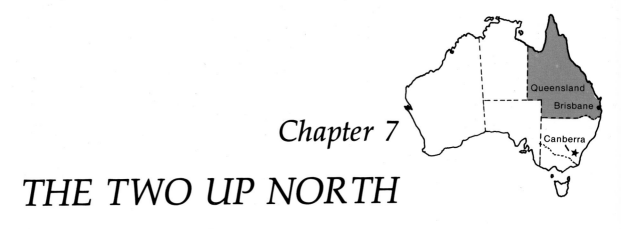

Chapter 7

THE TWO UP NORTH

There are two northern sections of the Commonwealth. One was the last to become a separate colony—Queensland. The other is still a territory—Northern Territory.

QUEENSLAND—THE SUNSHINE STATE

In 1606 the Dutch first sighted the western coast of Cape York. They considered the red cliffs unsuitable for colonizing.

In 1955 a geologist discovered that the red cliffs contained bauxite reserves. They are worth billions of dollars. The bauxite is mined and sent to Gladstone in southern Queensland for processing. Then it is shipped to the smelter at Bell Bay, Tasmania. There it becomes aluminum. There are other smelters at Geelong and Kwinana. Australia is the largest bauxite producer in the world.

The state is rich in other resources. Coal, iron ore, copper, uranium, tin, gold, silver, lead, and zinc are mined. Queensland is bisected by the Tropic of Capricorn. Its northern half is tropical, with large plantings of pineapple, sugarcane, citrus fruits, and tea. Oil and gas deposits have been found west of Brisbane, the capital. Pipelines bring these valuable resources to the city.

Brisbane is built on both sides of the Brisbane River.

Part of Queensland is north of the Tropic of Capricorn. The land receives almost direct rays of sun throughout the year. Temperatures get very hot.

Queensland's first settlement was a penal colony established in 1824. Twenty years later free settlers came north. They took up holdings on the rich pastoral lands to the west. After repeated requests from the settlers, the British government separated the region from New South Wales in December, 1859. Queensland, named in honor of Queen Victoria, became a separate colony, with Brisbane as its capital.

Queensland produces more beef for market than any other state. It ranks fifth in the production of sheep and wool.

Brisbane is built on both sides of the Brisbane River. There are narrow, congested streets in the older section. But there are many beautiful parks and gardens with tropical trees and plants. The clock tower of City Hall rises above King George Square. From its observation platform there is an excellent view of the city.

A good way to explore north of Brisbane is on the Sunshine Route, an air-conditioned train. The Great Dividing Range is a backdrop for the beautiful forests and farms along the way.

At Gladstone ships dock at the wharves to load grain, fish, meat, petroleum, chemicals, coal, and copper concentrates. They load bauxite for the smelter in Tasmania.

The southern end of the Great Barrier Reef is opposite Gladstone. Farther north is Rockhampton, the center of the beef industry. Dairying is also important here. The city lies almost exactly on the Tropic of Capricorn.

Harvesting sugarcane in Tully, south of Cairns in Queensland.

The tropical climate enables farmers to grow tropical fruits and sugarcane. Sugar mills produce raw sugar from which refined sugar is made. Australia is one of the world's largest producers of sugar.

Cairns is in the north of Queensland. Flowers grow everywhere. Beaches, big game fishing, and trips to the Great Barrier Reef attract tourists.

Queensland can be divided into four regions: the coastal strip, the mountains of the Great Dividing Range, the western tableland, and the semiarid plains of the Great Artesian Basin. Two tablelands, Darling Downs in the south and Atherton Tableland in the north, are fertile and productive. With enough rainfall the tablelands are well suited to agriculture.

The semiarid plains cover half of the state. The Great Artesian Basin is the largest in the world, 772,000 square miles (1,999,480 square kilometers). It is a saucer-shaped basin with the eastern rim higher than those on the south, west, and north. Rain in the Eastern Highlands of New South Wales and Queensland soaks into water-bearing layers, traveling to the western areas where rainfall is much less.

In some places the water comes up through natural outlets. On many cattle and sheep stations man-made bores provide outlets. In some places the water is so hot it must pass through cooling towers before it can be used. By 1970 there were 4,500 bores, 2,900 of which still operated. Twenty thousand shallower bores or wells yielded water by pumping. Plastic pipes are laid to conserve water for distribution to livestock on stations in arid and semiarid regions.

In 1844 Ludwig Leichhardt led an expedition from near Brisbane to the Gulf of Carpentaria and Arnhem Land in the Northern Territory and back. He discovered many rivers as well as land suitable for grazing. In 1848 Leichhardt set out again from near Brisbane. He planned to cross the continent. Perth was his goal. The expedition disappeared. No trace was found of Leichhardt or the men accompanying him. Search parties found only a few saddle horses.

THE NORTHERN TERRITORY—SO LARGE, YET SMALL

The Northern Territory comprises one sixth of the continent. It lies between Queensland and Western Australia and north of the

A modern section of Darwin

twenty-sixth parallel, the boundary with South Australia. It is now self-governing and eventually will achieve statehood. Darwin is the territory's capital. The area of the Northern Territory is twice the size of Texas, but its population was only about 130,000 in 1981. The northern region is called the Top End. Darwin has an average annual rainfall of 60 inches (1.5 meters). The average temperature in summer is 90 degrees Fahrenheit (32.2 degrees Celsius) and 75 degrees Fahrenheit (23.9 degrees Celsius) in winter.

Planned in 1869, Darwin now is the largest city and chief port in the Northern Territory.

During World War II, on February 19, 1942, Darwin was bombed by Japanese planes. Buildings were destroyed and 243 people were killed. Aussie and American soldiers poured into the area. Fortunately, Australia was not invaded.

On Christmas Day, 1974, much of Darwin again was leveled. This time a cyclone had struck. Now rebuilt, the city is a busy port. Ships travel to towns and cities along the coast and down to Perth. Other ships sail north to Asian ports. The city also has an international airport.

A camel train near Alice Springs

First surveyed in 1869, Darwin grew slowly. Communication with other parts of the country was difficult. Finally the Overland Telegraph Line was completed in 1872 between Darwin and Adelaide. During World War II the road between Darwin and Alice Springs was paved. Paving has been completed as far as the border with South Australia. From there to Port Augusta the road is gravel, but it is paved from Port Augusta to Adelaide.

Once a week the New Ghan, a train, makes its twenty-four-hour run between Adelaide and Alice Springs. It is named for the Afghans who drove camel trains across the arid center of the territory and Western Australia. One hundred camels were used to carry supplies for the construction of the Overland Telegraph Line. They also took supplies to mining towns and returned with ore. There were at least four thousand camels serving as pack animals in 1900. The railroad and trucks replaced the last camel caravan in 1930. Some camels still roam wild. Others are used by prospectors or for tourist interest.

THE ABORIGINALS IN THE NORTHERN TERRITORY

There are more than twenty-five thousand Aboriginals in the territory. Most of them live on land ceded to them through land rights legislation. Arnhem Land, east of Darwin, is a large Aboriginal reserve. In 1977 the Aboriginal Land Rights (Northern Territory) Act granted the Aboriginals ownership of reserves and other lands. This is 18.4 percent of the territory.

Copper, bauxite, and uranium have been found in Arnhem Land. Although the government holds the mineral rights, the land can be leased for mining with the approval of the Aboriginals. Money from these leases could amount to millions of dollars. This money would benefit all Northern Territory Aboriginals.

What is Aboriginal life like today? In the Northern Territory there are fifteen schools in which twelve Aboriginal languages are taught, along with English, in an attempt to preserve the culture of the people. There is no written form of the languages.

Throughout the country young Aboriginal children attend secondary schools while older students are in technical schools, universities, or adult education classes.

Many of the men work on cattle and other stations. Others are employed on community projects—road work, forestry, fisheries, building trades, and nursing, to improve the reserves. Some serve as aides in Aboriginal primary and secondary schools and as preschool assistants.

Nevertheless, Aboriginal unemployment is high. Frequently families live in remote areas or small communities where the jobs are limited. The government is making efforts to increase training and job opportunities.

An Aboriginal working on a banana plantation on Echo Island,
an island off the northern coast of Northern Australia

Many strange rock formations are found in the red center of Australia.

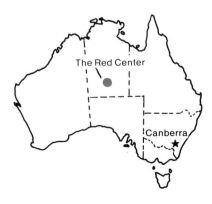

The Red Center

Canberra

ALICE SPRINGS—HALFWAY BETWEEN

Alice Springs lies in the red center halfway between Darwin and Adelaide. It was a supply base during World War II.

Tourism and the presence of Americans working in nearby research stations have accounted for an increase in population. In summer temperatures can reach 110 degrees Fahrenheit, (43.3 degrees Celsius) but at night in winter they can drop below freezing.

In 1927, a missionary, the Reverend John Flynn of the Australian Inland Mission, started an outback clinic in the Alice, as Alice Springs is often called. He urged the establishment of emergency medical service by airplane. It would provide help for people on isolated cattle stations. His suggestion became one of the most important contributions to the health and welfare of people in the outback. The Flying Doctor Service and Flying Ambulance Service began in 1928.

Through transceivers (two-way radios), people on remote sheep and cattle stations hundreds of miles from doctors receive medical advice. The radio base at Alice Springs covers an area of 440,000 square miles (1,139,600 square kilometers). The farthest station is 530 miles (853 kilometers) away. The base logs 100,000 miles (160,900 kilometers) on emergency flights a year. In addition, 80,000 miles (128,720 kilometers) of routine clinical flights are flown by the Royal Flying Doctor Service yearly.

The planes are equipped to serve as ambulances. Patients can be flown to the nearest hospital. Flying doctors can perform some surgery while on the planes or in the homes of injured or ill persons. Today there are twelve bases throughout the outback.

In Alice Springs the John Flynn Memorial Church is a tribute to the minister's contribution to the health of thousands of outback residents. Flynn died in 1951.

The School of the Air also has a station operating in the Alice. Started in 1951, it was the first radio school serving children in the outback. Pupils on remote cattle and sheep stations use transceivers to receive instruction and answer questions. When they participate in a play, the teacher records the program and plays it back for everyone to hear.

Cattle stations of several thousand square miles are not unusual. These stations have weekly mail delivery by plane. There are at least 110 landing strips in the territory serving stations and small settlements. The pilot mailman may fly many miles between landing strips. He picks up mail, including lessons from pupils, and delivers it to the city where he is based.

Alice Springs is a base for tours to the parks and reserves in central Australia. Uluru National Park is the most famous. It has strange formations, the peaks of a buried mountain range. The park preserves the culture of the Yankuntjatjara and Pitjantjatjara Aboriginal tribes.

Ewaninga Rock Carvings Conservation Reserve is a short distance south of Alice Springs. In the soft sandstone, Aboriginals carved numerous symbols. Their meanings, however, have been forgotten by the tribes.

Other tourist attractions that can be reached from the town include Simpson's Gap National Park, Trephina Gorge Nature Park, Finks Gorge National Park, and Henbury Meteorite Craters Conservation Reserve. Chambers Pilla, a historical reserve, is important in Aboriginal mythology.

An Aboriginal artist works in a cave on Wessel Island, an island off the northern coast of Northern Australia.

Australia leads the world in producing and exporting wool.

Chapter 8

SHEEP, CATTLE,
AND HARD WORK

Australia's economy has been built on agriculture since the time of the first colony at Sydney. Although the number of people engaged in rural industry has declined, production has risen significantly since 1946. Farmers use improved pasture and crop management. They apply fertilizers and trace elements where soils lack them. Irrigation and mechanization make farming more productive. More than 40 percent of Australia's export income comes from rural industry—farming and grazing.

SHEEP—ONE OF THE LEADING RURAL INDUSTRIES

The sheep Captain Phillip brought to Sydney Cove were intended to provide fresh meat. Their coats were hairlike, unsuited for wool. In 1794 John Macarthur, Isaac Nichols, and the Reverend Samuel Marsden began crossbreeding Bengal and Irish sheep to improve the wool.

In 1797 Captain Henry Waterhouse went to the Cape of Good Hope to buy cattle. He took twenty-six Spanish merino sheep back to the settlement. Fourteen survived the journey. Macarthur purchased several of them. The others were assigned to other sheep-farming colonists. By the early 1800s Macarthur had developed merinos with wool as fine as any Spanish wool. Soon Australia was exporting wool to Great Britain.

Sheep are grazed in three broad zones. The largest zone has the most unpredictable annual rainfall, averaging from 5 to 15 inches (127 to 381 millimeters). Twenty-three percent of the country's sheep graze here. Often a station must have 50 acres (20 hectares) of grassland per sheep. Such sheep stations must be very large.

The second zone is an area where there is sufficient rainfall to raise wheat and other grains as well as to graze sheep. Farmers in this zone rotate crops on their land. This helps prevent soil erosion. Forty-four percent of Australia's sheep are raised in this zone.

The finest wool is produced in the third zone, the high rainfall area. Here one third of Australia's sheep are raised. Lambs are fattened for slaughter. These sheep stations may also raise cattle. They are smaller runs than those in the other zones. Where rainfall is less, sheep require a much larger run. Flocks or "mobs" in high rainfall areas may number as high as two thousand sheep.

Of Australia's 66,000 sheep-raising properties, those in southwestern Victoria are among the finest. Operating a sheep station takes hard work. Often a few men and their well-trained dogs handle all of the work on thousands of acres of fenced paddocks. Miles and miles of fences must be kept in repair. The fences keep out kangaroos and wallabies. Sometimes special fences that keep out rabbits and dingoes are necessary. Owners must be sure that the sheep are kept in their own runs. The men ride horseback or drive motorbikes or utility trucks.

Natural grasses provide feed for many of the country's sheep and lambs. Some stations improve the soil and

Australia is the driest continent. Dams, such as the Cotter River Dam, have been built to store water to be used during the dry season.

grasses by spreading fertilizers from airplanes. Phosphate mined in New South Wales and the Northern Territory and chemical fertilizers are used. Certain elements, such as zinc, copper, and manganese, are added if tests show they are lacking.

Rye, clover, and other natural grasses provide feed on many stations. Oats and baled hay are fed to ewes before lambs are born.

Water is necessary wherever sheep graze. They are unable to go without water for more than four days. In southeastern New South Wales, water from the Snowy Mountains Hydroelectric Scheme is directed westward into storage areas behind dams. The water passes through tunnels to generating stations and then on to rivers west of the Great Dividing Range. Farmers and graziers benefit from a dependable water supply. In areas too far from lakes or rivers, man-made water holes or troughs fed by artesian bores provide much-needed water.

Skilled shearers travel from station to station, so mustering is carried on at different times. Mustering is like a roundup of sheep. Shearing is done yearly. Without shearing in the hot climate of many runs, sheep would die of the heat. Ticks, lice, and itch mites would attack them.

It is important to muster the ewes before the lambs are born. The ewes receive a vaccine that protects both them and their lambs from a disease called pulpy kidney.

Sheep in the paddock are widely scattered. They are mustered into small flocks and then into a "mob." They are then driven down to the shearing shed.

Most of the shearers use mechanical clippers. Holding a sheep up with its head in the shearer's lap, he first shears the belly and the dirty, useless wool on the inside of the legs. Then quickly he removes the good fleece off the sheep's back in one piece. A good shearer can handle at least 120 sheep in a day.

The whole fleece is thrown on a table. The rough, dirty edges are removed. A wool classer determines its grade. The average weight of a fleece is 9.5 pounds (4.3 kilograms). A top merino ram may have as much as 55 pounds (25 kilograms) of wool.

Each grade is baled separately. The bales are marked on the outside with their quality and the station's brand. The wool is very greasy. After the grease has been removed and purified, it becomes lanolin. Lotions and cosmetics often contain lanolin.

Most wool is sold at auctions in various centers throughout the country. Buyers from all over the world come to bid on the fine wool. Japan, Russia, China, and the European Economic Community countries are principal markets. Some wool is used in Australia's own spinning and weaving factories.

Sometimes when shearing is completed a grazier and his family will plan a barbecue for the shearers. Neighbors who live many miles away may attend. The men barbecue lamb chops and steaks. The women bring dishes filled with their favorite foods. The wife of the grazier prepares even more food. Adults and children enjoy these rare times together with neighbors they see so seldom.

Shearing sheep

Merinos produce excellent wool. They are not good meat animals. More than thirty-two million sheep and lambs are slaughtered yearly for domestic and foreign consumption. Usually these are crossbreeds. Some crossbreeds not only produce good quality wool for carpets but are good meat animals as well.

Australia produces more sheep than any other country. It ships live animals to other countries. In 1980 almost six million were sent to Middle Eastern countries.

The number of sheep has declined in recent years. Nevertheless, wool, together with wheat and meat production, make up the country's most important rural industries.

CATTLE

Several years after the First Fleet landed, the cattle brought for the colony were found wandering some distance away. Another small herd arrived in 1791. By 1800 there were more than one thousand cows and bulls. By 1815 New South Wales was a dairying center.

As new grazing land was discovered, cattle were brought overland to new stations. It was no easy task for drovers to move cattle across land with little vegetation and water. But by the 1880s cattle drives of long distances brought cattle to market.

In the one hundred years between 1868 and 1968 there were eight major droughts. The droughts caused severe losses in the cattle industry. In the 1964/1965 drought a million cattle died of hunger and thirst or had to be slaughtered. Cattle stations had water and feed only for small herds.

Beef cattle graze on more than one hundred and fifty thousand properties. Where there is enough water, sheep also graze. Wheat

A cattle auction in New South Wales

and other grains are grown to provide additional feed for the animals.

New South Wales has more than fifty thousand cattle stations. Victoria ranks second. The Northern Territory has few cattle runs because they must be extremely large to provide enough grass for each animal.

Some Americans have purchased large tracts of land on the southern coast of Western Australia. They have established sheep and cattle stations. On Orleans Farm, for example, fifty-two thousand sheep and one thousand Santa Gertrudis cattle grazed on only 16,000 acres (6,400 hectares) by 1971. Good grazing land improves the quality and amount of wool on sheep and the beef per heifer or steer. The Santa Gertrudis cattle came from the King Ranch in Texas. They are a cross between the humped Brahman of India and the Shorthorn.

The oldest Northern Territory run had seventy thousand head on 5,000,000 acres (2,025,000 hectares). Cattle roamed freely and unrestricted. Fencing on large properties was nonexistent.

Breeding was uncontrolled. The land was overgrazed. The soil eroded and became useless.

Such large properties are being reduced to improve management. The largest station is 6,290 square miles (16,300 square kilometers). The typical station is only 1,300 square miles (3,367 square kilometers), with fenced paddocks. Breeding is controlled to improve the pastures. Tick control is strongly enforced. Cattle must pass inspection for ticks if they are shipped into "clean country."

The stockman is in charge of mustering or cattle roundup. He must be a man of many talents and abilities. He must be an excellent horseman and be able to drive a truck hundreds of miles over rough terrain in search of cattle. He also should be able to perform veterinary tasks. Cattle need inoculations against disease which could wipe them out. During mustering he must select the finest male calves for herd bulls and cull animals of poor quality. It is his job to decide which animals should be driven to market.

Drovers are often Aboriginals. Their work is very important in driving a thousand or more head long distances. The cattle must be kept in good condition even though they may go without water for two days or more.

Stockmen and drovers herd the cattle. They drive them to coastal pastures for fattening. From there the cattle are taken to packing plants near seaports. Much of Australia's beef from the semidesert region is exported to the United States.

The station owner or manager often flies light planes over the station looking for lost animals or checking the pasture.

Even on large stations with seventy-five thousand head, only two or three boundary riders are needed. They ride alongside the fences on horseback. They check for breaks and remove brush that has been caught in the fences. By clearing the brush they prevent bushfires. A fencer and his assistant follow along in a small truck or wagon pulled by a donkey. They repair the breaks.

Station horses are very important. The men choose the finest, often importing them. Paddocks for the horses are near the station buildings. Some stations have a blacksmith to shoe horses and make other repairs. With the nearest town perhaps more than 100 miles (161 kilometers) away, skilled workers are needed on the stations.

DAIRYING

Most dairy farms are in temperate regions with good rainfall. The eastern and southern fertile lands near the coast of the mainland states and northern Tasmania are major dairying areas. Irrigated areas farther inland in Victoria are new dairylands.

One third of the milk supply is used in butter making. Although almost two thirds of the butter is consumed by Australians, more than 37,000 tons (35,566 metric tonnes) are exported each year. Cheese and powdered milk also are exported.

Dairy farms are much smaller than beef cattle stations. Many dairy farmers also raise pigs and hogs. Japan imports a small amount of Australian pork. Poultry, more than 90 percent chickens, is increasing in popularity on Australian tables. Consumption of dressed poultry increased by almost 30 percent in the past five years. The principal markets for poultry exports are Papua New Guinea and islands in the Pacific.

GRAINS, FRUITS, AND VEGETABLES

Grain plantings began with the first settlers. Today the country

Modern machinery is used to harvest crops.

raises over 16,000,000 tons (14,515,000 metric tonnes) of wheat for grain. Much of this is exported. A large quantity of the wheat is raised on land that was considered unsuited for crops not long ago.

In the district around Esperance, a seaport on the southern coast of Western Australia, farmers raise "shandy," a mixture of wheat and oats for hay. It is fed to Polled Hereford cattle. At Esperance Downs Research Station scientists study crop rotation and ways to improve soil conditions. They have found that by fertilizing with superphosphate mixed with trace elements of zinc, copper, and cobalt the soil is made more fertile. Crop production increases.

Nine percent of all used land in Australia is cultivated for agriculture and intensive grazing. In some states wheat depends on winter rains. In others, spring rains are essential. Moisture retained from summer rains in northern New South Wales and in Queensland supports wheat and other grains. A serious drought in 1972 reduced the country's total production drastically.

Wheat farms require few people for their operation. Plowing and sowing are done mechanically. Modern harvesters move through the fields of ripened grain cutting, thrashing, and bagging seed. Some of the crop is blown into silos for future planting or for livestock feed. Most will be hauled by truck to concrete grain elevators. The grain elevators are along railroad sidings. Sometimes the grain is taken directly to a seaport like Fremantle.

Long wheat trains carry the grain to ports where enormous elevators hold it for loading into oceangoing ships. Wheat is shipped to Japan, the People's Republic of China, Russia, Egypt, and Southeast Asia countries.

The irrigated fields of New South Wales and Queensland produce rice for home and foreign consumption. Papua New Guinea, Indonesia, and Hong Kong are the principal importers of Australian rice.

The sugarcane fields of Queensland are very productive. Australia is able to compete on the world sugar market through its scientific cane breeding, cultivation, disease control, and harvesting techniques. Higher yields are achieved than in other tropical countries.

Machines chop the cane into short lengths. A dip in a mercurial solution protects them from insects. The machine plants each piece, fertilizes it, and tamps down the soil over it. When the stalks are 12 to 15 feet (3.7 to 4.6 meters) tall, they have lovely plumes or flowers. It is time to cut the cane mechanically. The cane is hauled to a raw sugar refinery. In large terminals the raw sugar awaits shipment to many markets, including the United States where it is refined into white crystals.

Only 1 percent of the area in cultivated crops is used for fruit raising. Nevertheless, fruits and berries account for 11 percent of

Bananas and citrus fruits are grown in Queensland.

the value of the principal crops produced. Apples are now the most valuable crop. Oranges, pears, peaches, apricots, plums, pineapples, bananas, grapes, and berries are sold fresh, canned, or frozen. Canneries and frozen food factories also process vegetables—beans, peas, corn, carrots, and tomatoes. Australians enjoy fresh fruits and vegetables all year round.

MINERALS AND MINING

William Dampier explored the Indian Ocean coast of the continent north of the Tropic of Capricorn in 1699. The land was worthless, he thought. But 250 years later large cattle stations flourished on the semiarid plains.

During the Christmas holidays in 1952, Lang Hancock, who operated two cattle stations and did a little mining, flew south from the outback to visit friends. A storm forced him low over the Hamersley Range. He guided his small plane through a river gorge. The reddish walls appeared to be iron ore. Four months later Hancock returned to the gorge. "I took samples," he said. "I realized this was a major discovery."

Not until 1961 did Hancock receive a title for prospecting and developing the iron ore deposits. In the early sixties the government lifted a ban on the export of iron ore. Mount Tom Price was a mountain of iron ore.

Now giant shovels bite into the mountain. They scoop up high-grade ore-laden ground and load it into large trucks. It is hot, dirty work for the strip miners. After work they return to the township of Tom Price with its air-conditioned homes, green lawns, and gardens. Their families have everything they need in the town. There are times, however, when strong winds blow hot and dry, whipping the red soil over everything.

The truckers drive their loads to the railhead on a railway built especially for the mine. Dampier is the new port 182 miles (293 kilometers) away. It, too, has a pleasant township for the workers. Ore carriers are loaded and sail for distant ports. Much of the ore goes to Japanese steel mills.

The iron ore deposits in Western Australia are thought to be among the largest in the world. There are several other mountains in the region that have rich ore deposits. At Port Hedland a new port handles iron ore shipments from these mines.

Off the coast of Dampier on Barrow Island four-man crews have drilled hundreds of wells. The unrefined oil produced is piped to separator stations where gas is separated from it. The oil then is pumped to holding tanks near the shore. A pipeline that can be seen only at low tide carries the oil 6 miles (9.5 kilometers) out to sea to waiting tankers.

The roustabouts, as oil field workers are known, live on the island. They fly down to Perth on their weeks off. Geologists have found oil offshore north of Barrow Island. Bass Strait is Australia's largest oil field. There is another large oil and gas development on

The remains of a crushing plant where gold was found around 1870

the northwest shelf of Western Australia. Australia is about 70 percent self-sufficient in oil.

Across the country in Queensland, Mount Isa produces copper, silver, lead, and zinc. These mines are deep underground. The city of Mount Isa near the mines is modern despite the long distance from major cities. Townsville, 567 miles (912 kilometers) east, ships supplies by train or plane to the mining families. Since the rainfall is less than 16 inches (41 centimeters) annually, it is difficult to raise crops.

The copper smelter at Mount Isa processes the ore into blister copper. Shipped to Townsville, the blister copper is refined and exported or used in Australia's factories.

Mount Isa is the site of a station of the Royal Flying Doctor Service. It services Queensland and part of the Northern Territory. The radio operated by the base doctor is also used by the School of the Air. Teachers instruct students, who are also enrolled in the Primary Correspondence School.

Gold was discovered in 1851 in New South Wales near Bathurst and later at Hill End. The great gold rush that followed matched the one in California. Thousands of people came to Australia to make a fortune. Today gold mining is carried on in some degree in all of the states except Victoria.

Coal mining in Victoria

Australia has 17 percent of the world's uranium reserves. Brown coal, or lignite, is mined in open cuts in Victoria. Bucket-wheel dredgers dig the coal out on deepening terraces. Conveyors carry the coal to rail lines. Some is used in generating stations. Much of it is sent to briquette plants where the coal is pressed into small bricks of fuel.

Australia's opals, discovered in 1911 in Coober Pedy, are popular gemstones. They are mined in only a few areas of South Australia and New South Wales.

Opal mining is very different from copper mining. It is slow and laborious. Twenty-four tons of copper ore reach the surface in each automated skip. Thirty skips are filled each hour. Opals are mined at Coober Pedy and Andamooka in the desert of South Australia and at Lightening Ridge in New South Wales.

Huge deposits of black coal are mined in New South Wales and Queensland. Black coal is one of Australia's largest export earners.

BUSINESS AND THE BIG CITIES

Australia's population has doubled since 1945. Over 75 percent of the people live in cities. Two thirds of the population is in the capital cities, including Canberra. As farmers use more mechanized equipment, more people move into urban areas seeking employment. In 1947, more than 18 percent of the labor force was engaged in agriculture, forestry, and fishing. The figure had dropped to less than 7 percent by 1977.

Australia is rapidly becoming self-sufficient. Its factories produce clothing, shoes, textiles, cars and trucks, household appliances, beverages, paper products, furniture, carpets, and chemicals.

Other people find employment in sales, services, and sports and recreation.

Each year more than one hundred thousand homes and thirty thousand other buildings are constructed. Australians prefer single-family homes. Following World War II there was a housing shortage. More than two million new homes and apartments were built in the building boom that followed. In the cities brick houses are built. In rural areas the homes are frame (wood).

In 1980, Australia exported more than she imported. The value of exports was $2.5 million more than the imports. Japan and the United States are the country's primary markets. Australia purchases most of its imports from the United States, Japan, the United Kingdom, other European countries, New Zealand, Saudi Arabia (oil), and ASEAN (the Association of South East Asian Nations) countries.

Australia carries on trade with two hundred countries. Most of the ships that serve its ports are foreign-flag vessels. However, the country is adding to its merchant fleet.

The country cooperates with its nearest neighbors—Malaysia, Singapore, New Zealand, and Papua New Guinea—in defense. It also maintains an alliance with the United States and New Zealand.

For one hundred years the United States and Australia have cooperated in scientific projects.

The Australian standard of living is high. Its economy is growing in agriculture, mining, transportation, manufacturing, service jobs, and the financial sector. Its major problem is distance. Australia is thousands of miles from Europe and North and South America. It is also handicapped by the distance across a broad expanse of arid land. Modern transportation and communication have helped to bridge this distance.

AUSTRALIA'S ROLE IN THE WORLD COMMUNITY

Australia is recognized as a medium-sized power in international affairs. Its delegates to the San Francisco conference in June, 1945, signed the Charter of the United Nations. It has membership on several UN commissions and agencies.

Through ASEAN, the country promotes regional cooperation with Southeast Asian govenments. Economic growth and political stability are major concerns of ASEAN.

Over thirty countries belong to the Commonwealth of Nations. They are independent nations formerly under British rule. Australia was host to a meeting of the heads of Commonwealth governments in 1981.

Above: Some Australians enjoy a picnic while they look over Lake Burley Griffin in Canberra.
Below: A home in surburban New South Wales

Chapter 9

LIVING, LEISURE,
AND LEARNING

When the British settled at Sydney Cove, they could not possibly dream of the future importance of the continent. Today, were it not for cars that drive on the left side of the road, Sydney is like any large American or Canadian city.

Most of the city's workers live away from the commercial center in the suburbs. One-story houses with red-tiled roofs stand on individual lots. Often these five-room bungalows have a veranda or porch.

In the warmer climate of Brisbane, many houses are built on stilts. Cooling breezes can blow through under them. Garages are under the houses. Roofing is often corrugated iron.

Canberra is considered a model city. It has broad avenues, no pollution, and a beautiful uncluttered appearance. There are no billboards or fences. Utility wires are underground.

Since World War II more than 3.5 million immigrants have entered the country. Usually they settle in communities where they can share ethnic and cultural backgrounds with others from their homelands. This is especially true in Sydney and Melbourne. They have their own ethnic clubs, sports activities, churches, and food preferences. Immigrants have contributed a depth and richness to Australia's life.

Lifesaving clubs

Farther from the coast and in the outback are small towns. They provide services to people who may live very long distances away and come to town on rare visits. A few small industries exist in some towns. Often there are few tourist attractions.

Modern mining towns are like small oases. They provide all of the workers' needs. Old mining towns became ghost towns. With a revival in mining recently, some old buildings have been put to good use. The large sandstone buildings stand along wide main streets.

City dwellers frequently own "weekender" homes along the Pacific coast north and south of Sydney. These small houses make it possible for them to enjoy the sunny beaches. In Queensland, Surfers Paradise and the Gold Coast south of Brisbane attract residents and tourists.

Surf lifesavers patrol beaches, ready to push their lightweight five-man boats into the waves. They row out to rescue persons in distress. There are 250 lifesaving clubs with 25,000 volunteers. They hold contests to test their speed and skill. They have saved more than 150,000 persons through the years.

Tourists and vacationers can enjoy the many national parks and reserves in Australia.

Many coast dwellers never have crossed the Great Dividing Range and visited the outback. They do enjoy the city zoos, national parks and nature reserves, and animal and bird sanctuaries. Every state has parks and reserves. Wisely, Australia protects its wildlife.

Australians who live along the coast spend much of their free time boating or enjoying boat races.

Water sports are popular. Australian Olympic swimmers have captured many medals in the games. Australians also enjoy surfboarding, sailing, speed boating, and fishing.

With ideal climate along the coast, people spend as much time outdoors as possible. Many local teams participate in cricket. National teams from Australia, the United Kingdom, India, Pakistan, New Zealand, and the West Indies compete in test matches. The Australian teams have won more often than most of their opponents.

Summer is the best time for tennis. Eight thousand tennis clubs exist. There are thousands of courts. Margaret Court and Evonne Goolagong Cawley, an Aboriginal, have won the tournament at Wimbledon, England. Famous male competitors include Rod Laver, John Newcombe, and Ken Rosewall.

Both fans and athletes enjoy rugby, soccer, and Australian Rules football. These are winter sports. Basketball and boxing attract thousands of spectators indoors.

In the 1896 Olympics Edwin Flack won medals in the 800-meter and 1,500-meter races. There was not yet an Australian flag to raise in honor of his achievements. Since then the country's flag has been raised for many events in track and field, swimming, cycling, rowing, and other sports that have been won by Australian Olympians.

Many people play golf. Australian golfers compete in international championship contests. Many have been champions.

THE ARTS

The fine arts and performing arts are supported enthusiastically in Australia. For the first hundred years, artists and writers followed British and European traditions. The rise in nationalism between 1880 and World War II increased Australian identity. Since then the works of creative artists and writers have gained worldwide recognition.

It is fortunate that artists painted landscapes of early Australia. There were no cameras to record those scenes. The artists left a picture of life at that time. By 1861 Melbourne built the first public gallery in Australia. Other capital cities followed shortly thereafter.

The Heidelberg School of Australian Painting, named for a suburb of Melbourne, influenced artists depicting their land. The school was founded by Tom Roberts, Arthur Streeton, and Frederick McCubbin.

American architecture influenced house designs. The California-style bungalow and the Spanish Mission style with tile roofs and cement walls became popular in the 1920s. Now an international style is used.

For many years the theater depended largely upon performers and plays from the United States and Great Britain. Finally native playwrights began to write about their own land. Their works employed Australia's own actors and actresses.

Many fine musicians, composers, and singers have developed in the country. Often they spend a period away from their homeland but return for performances. Nellie Melba, a great opera star, and Percy Grainger, a composer and pianist, gained international fame many years ago.

Opera is very popular today. The Australian Opera, a national company, and the Australian Ballet Foundation perform at home and in other countries. Smaller opera companies and orchestras are based in major cities.

Joan Sutherland is considered one of the world's finest sopranos. The Sydney Opera House is a symbol of the country's achievement in the arts.

ABORIGINAL ARTS

In many sections of the country, early Aboriginals left rock paintings and carvings. Some in the Northern Territory were done 20,000 to 25,000 years ago. Aboriginals believe these red, yellow, white, and black paintings were creative beings from Dreamtime who entered caves and became paintings.

Bark paintings are so popular that modern Aboriginal artists produce them for sale. They are made from large pieces of eucalyptus bark dried flat, treated, and then painted. Originally they decorated the shelters of the coastal tribes. A famous Aboriginal artist who worked in water colors was Albert Namatjira. Many other traditional artists are gaining recognition for their work on bark and artifacts.

There are other famous Aboriginals in the art world—Harold Blair, a singer; Kath Walker, poet; and David Gulpilil, dancer and actor. Bella Malina is an artist who paints many of the native birds. The Ella brothers, who are rugby players, and Lionel Rose, a world boxing champion, have done well in sports.

LEARNING ON MANY LEVELS

Education is compulsory between the ages of six and fifteen. Preschools are open in many cities. Children are admitted to primary school at five years of age. They attend until they are about twelve years old. Seventh through twelfth grades are held

A primary school

in high school. Special education facilities, open-space schools, and vocational education are available.

A Year 10 Certificate, like a diploma, is issued when a student completes that year. Even the student's grades are listed. Two more years, years 11 and 12, also are provided in secondary education.

By 1982 there were over 160,000 students attending Australia's nineteen universities. Still more attend colleges of advanced education for degree courses and diplomas. Ten universities train doctors. There are about twenty-seven thousand doctors throughout the country.

Often the Royal Flying Doctor Service shares its two-way radio operation with the School of the Air. In some places the School of the Air has its own transmitting and receiving wavelengths. The twelve schools serve primary school students.

Each teacher has about forty students. A large school has four broadcasting studios. Four teachers can broadcast at the same time.

Pupils in the same grade tune in at the same time. They may live hundreds of miles apart. Often their home transmitters are battery powered. The broadcast signals are too weak to be heard in other homes. Group discussion is impossible during the thirty-minute-long lessons. Only one child at a time can answer or ask a question. However, each child does have some time for individual instruction.

The children also are enrolled in the Correspondence School. When the plane stops with mail at the cattle and sheep stations, the children's homework is picked up and carried to their teachers.

The Correspondence School offers education from kindergarten to year twelve. However, most students move to the city for years seven to twelve, where they stay with relatives or friends, or at boarding school.

School of the Air teachers try to make their pupils feel they are in a regular classroom. They arrange an outing or picnic in a central location. It is a pleasant occasion for the children to meet each other and their teachers. The School of the Air helps to reduce the isolation felt by rural children. It brings them in contact with other children.

The government operates over 7,500 schools. There are more than two thousand nongovernment or private schools. Usually they are sponsored by church groups.

Many immigrant children enter school. The government provides emergency funding to help these children, especially refugees, adjust to school.

Australia's educational programs are a challenge. The students come from many different cultures and backgrounds. Many live far from school buildings. The achievements of many of its university graduates are outstanding.

ACHIEVEMENTS AND AWARDS

The quality of education and research in universities has made Australia a leader in the arts, science, and medicine. The Australian Academy of Science includes leaders in physical and biological sciences. Five Australian scientists have been honored with Nobel Prizes in chemistry, physics, and medicine.

The continent's location in the Southern Hemisphere has given it an important role in space research. Space flight tracking stations operated in cooperation with United States' NASA (National Aeronautical and Space Administration) are located in South Australia and the Australian Capital Territory. These stations, manned by skilled scientists, provide communication with American astronauts. Skylab fell out of orbit over Australia. Fortunately it landed in a remote area. Viking projects and the space shuttle also are tracked. Australia also has launched its own satellites.

Australian authors have received international recognition, too. Patrick White received the Nobel Prize in literature in 1973. His novels, plays, and short stories about life in his country are widely acclaimed. Morris West has written several best-sellers. Thomas Keneally is considered one of Australia's finest writers.

Stretches of rocky cliffs can be found along the coast in New South Wales.

RESPONSIBILITIES FOR THE FUTURE

Australia's foreign policy places a major importance on ANZUS, the alliance between Australia, New Zealand, and the United States. Cultural relations encourage exchange programs in the arts, sports, and academic studies.

Papua New Guinea was a trust territory of Australia until it received independence in September, 1975. Papua New Guinea receives almost half of Australia's foreign aid funds.

Australia was one of the twelve original signers of the Antarctic Treaty in 1959. The Commonwealth claims more than one fourth of Antarctica. There are three Australian stations on the Antarctic continent and one on Macquarie Island. Scientists at these four stations conduct research in marine science, biology, medical sciences, glaciology, the upper atmosphere, and weather. The research is exchanged with other countries.

Achievements have been made through improved education, research facilities, and hospital services. Its great natural wealth and resourceful people are making Australia a leader not only in Southeast Asia and the South Pacific but in the entire world.

Lowercase letters refer to map inserts.

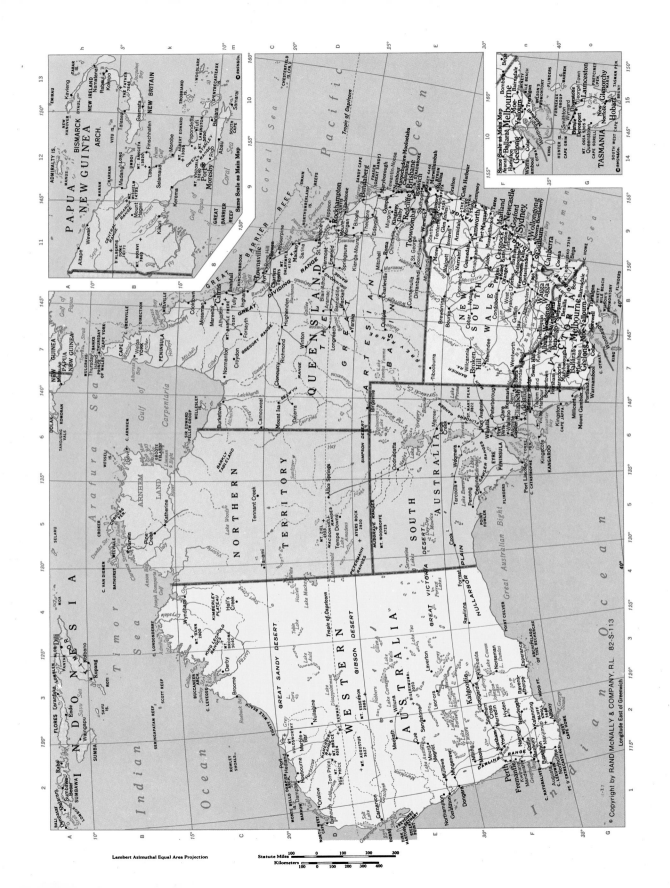

PAPUA NEW GUINEA

BISMARCK ARCH.

NEW IRELAND
NEW BRITAIN

Same Scale as Main Map

INDONESIA

NEW GUINEA
PAPUA NEW GUINEA

ARAFURA Sea

NORTHERN TERRITORY

QUEENSLAND

WESTERN AUSTRALIA

SOUTH AUSTRALIA

NEW SOUTH WALES

VICTORIA

Canberra

Melbourne

GREAT AUSTRALIAN BIGHT

Indian Ocean

Pacific Ocean

Coral Sea

Tasman Sea

TASMANIA

Hobart

Same Scale as Main Map

Tropic of Capricorn

Lambert Azimuthal Equal Area Projection

Statute Miles
100   0   100   200   300

Kilometers
100   0   100 200 300 400

© Copyright by RAND McNALLY & COMPANY, R.L. 82-S-113

Longitude East of Greenwich

MINI-FACTS AT A GLANCE

GENERAL INFORMATION

Official Name: Commonwealth of Australia

Other Names: The Dutch called it New Holland. Captain Cook named it New South Wales. Ptolemy, the Greek philosopher, called it *Terra Australis Incognita* (the Unknown Southern Land).

Capital: Canberra (Australian Capital Territory)

Official Language: English

Other Languages: Many languages are spoken by Aboriginal tribes.

Government: Australia is an independent self-governing nation. The prime minister is the head of the government. The queen of England is also the queen of Australia. The governor-general is the queen's representative. The Australian Parliament is made up of 64 members of the Senate and 125 members of the House of Representatives. Senators are elected to six-year terms. Representatives are elected three-year terms. All citizens eighteen years of age or older must vote or they can be fined. Each state has a state governor.

Flag: The flag is red, white, and blue. It has a small British Union Jack, five small stars for the constellation Southern Cross, and a large star for Australia.

Coat of Arms: The coat of arms has a kangaroo, an emu, and wattle blossoms. It also has a star for Australia and a shield with the states' coats of arms.

National Song: "Advance Australia Fair;" Royal anthem, "God Save the Queen."

Religion: There is no official religion. There is religious freedom. About 66 percent of the people are Protestants. About 27 percent are Roman Catholics. About 1 percent are Jewish. About 6 percent belong to other religions.

Money: Dollar and cents. One Australian dollar was worth about $1.00 in United States money in June 1989. Paper bills are issued in units of $1, $2, $5, $10, $20, and $50. Coins are issued in units of 1¢, 2¢, 5¢, 10¢, 20¢, and 50¢.

Weights and Measures: Australia uses the metric system.

Population: (All figures based on estimates by the Australian Bureau of Statistics,) 1990 estimate: 16,804,000—over 100,000 immigrants arrive each year.

States:

New South Wales	5,581,300
Victoria	4,188,300
Queensland	2,616,300
Western Australia	1,458,700
South Australia	1,378,900
Tasmania	448,600

Estimates for states and cities are 1988 estimates.

Over 85 percent of the people in Australia live in cities.

Cities: The ten largest cities are:

Sydney, New South Wales	3,430,000
Melbourne, Victoria	2,942,000
Brisbane, Queensland	1,171,000
Adelaide, South Austrialia	993,000
Perth, Western Austrialia	1,000,000
Newcastle, New South Wales	420,000
Canberra	267,600
Wollongong, New South Wales	no estimate
Hobart, Tasmania	190,000
Geelong, Victoria	no estimate

GEOGRAPHY

Australia is an island. It is also a continent. No other country in the world occupies an entire continent. It is the oldest, smallest, lowest, flattest continent in the world.

Highest Point: Mount Kosciusko, 7,310 ft. (2,228 m)

Lowest Point: Lake Eyre, 52 ft. (16 m) below sea level.

Rivers: The Murray River is the longest permanent river. It flows for 1,600 mi. (2,570 km). The Darling River flows for 1,700 mi. (2,740 km), but it is dry most of the year. Many rivers carry great amounts of water in the rainy season but are dry the rest of the year.

Lakes: Australia has no natural permanent lakes. Most lakes are dry for months or even years. The largest natural lakes are Lake Eyre, Lake Torrens, Lake Gairdner, and Lake Frome. The largest artificial lakes are Lake Argyle and Lake Gordon.

Mountains: The tallest mountains are found in the Australian Alps. The highest peak is Mount Kosciusko. Many of Australia's tall mountains are covered by snow in winter.

Deserts: About one third of Australia is desert covered.

Forests: About 105,000,000 a. (42,500,000 ha) of land is forest.

Coral Reef: The Great Barrier Reef is the longest coral reef in the world. It is 1,200 mi. (1,931 km) long. Australia has a total of 600 coral reefs. There are 340 species of coral in Australia.

Climate: Australia is usually warm and dry. There is no extreme cold and very little frost. It snows only in Tasmania and the Australian Alps. January mean temperature in Melbourne is 68° F. (20° C.). January mean temperature in Darwin is 84° F. (29° C.). Winter lasts from June to August. Summer lasts from December to February. Half of the country receives less than 10 in. (25 cm) of rain each year. Along the seacoasts the winds are strong and there have been cyclones.

Greatest Distances:
East to west—2,475 mi. (3,983 km)
North to south—1,950 mi. (3,138 km)

Area: Total: 2,966,150 sq. mi. (7,682,300 km²)

States:
New South Wales................. 309,500 sq. mi. (801,600 km²)
Queensland...................... 666,900 sq. mi. (1,727,200 km²)
South Australia .... 379,900 sq. mi. (984,000 km²)
Tasmania....................... 26,200 sq. mi. (67,800 km²)
Victoria .... 87,900 sq. mi. (227,600 km²)
Western Australia .... 975,100 sq. mi. (2,525,500 km²)

Mainland Territories:
Australian Capital Territory .... 930 sq. mi. (2,400 km²)
Northern Territory .... 519,700 sq. mi. (1,346,000 km²)

NATURE

Trees: The eucalyptus is the most common tree in Australia. There are 450 distinct forms of eucalyptus in Australia. Acacias, or wattles, can either be tall trees or shrubs. Australia has 700 species of acacias, 468 of which are indigenous to Australia. Other types of trees in Australia include palms, grass trees, macrozamia trees, kauri pine, bunya pine, baobab, blackwood, red cedar, coachwood, jarrah, Queensland maple, silky oak, and walnut.

Flowers: Western Australia is called the wild flower state because over two thousand species of flowers can be found there. There are 470 varieties of orchids in Australia. Other flowers include Christmas bush, desert pea, flanner flower, Geraldton wax plant, kangaroo paw, pomaderris, and waratah.

Birds: Two large birds, the emu and the cassowary, cannot fly. Australia is the only country that has black swans. The kookaburra, the best-known bird in Australia, is a member of the kingfisher family. Six hundred known resident species of birds live in Australia, including sixty different species of parrots. Other birds include anhinga, bellbird, bowerbird, galah, lyrebird, fairy penguin, rosella, cockatoo, hawk, and eagle.

Animals: About four hundred kinds of animals are native to Australia. Most of these are marsupials. There are about 150 species of marsupials in Australia. There are about fifty different species of kangaroos. Australia has a unique egg-laying mammal, the platypus. There are no hoofed animals or members of the cat family or primates native to Australia. Water buffalo, camels, rabbits, horses, and pigs were brought to Australia from other countries. Many of these animals now roam wild in the countryside. There are 370 kinds of lizards found in Australia. They are all nonpoisonous. Most of Australia's 140 species of snakes are poisonous.

Endangered Species: Some of Australia's animals are protected by law. These include six species of wallabies, three species of kangaroo rats, three species of parrots, three species of parakeets, three species of western whipbirds, and three species of crocodiles.

EVERYDAY LIFE

Food: Immigrants from Italy, Greece, Hungary, and other countries have brought with them spicy dishes. A typical dinner consists of roasted meat, such as beef or lamb, potatoes, and another vegetable. For snacks, Australians eat meat pies. They call french fries "chips." In summer many Australian families cook outdoors on barbecue grills.

Homes: Early settlers from Europe built houses from acacia branches and plaster. Ancient Aboriginal tribes did not build permanent homes. In winter their houses were made of bark shaped like a tent or A-frame. In the rainy season they built houses called "wurleys," which looked like beehives. A modern Australian house is one story, with five rooms, a porch, and a tile roof. In warm areas houses are built on stilts so breezes can cool the house. These houses have a garage underneath. Many people who live in cities have weekend houses in the beach areas.

Culture: The government helps to support the opera, ballet, theater, symphonic music, and motion picture industry. The National Library of Australia has more than three million books. Each state capital has a public art gallery. Australia has a national opera company and a national ballet company. Each state capital has a theater company. Australia has been producing motion pictures since 1900.

Holidays:
 January 1, New Year's Day
 January 26, Australia Day
 Good Friday
 Easter Sunday
 Easter Monday
 April 25, Anzac Day
 May 24, Commonwealth Day
 December 25, Christmas Day
 December 26, Boxing Day
 Labor Day is a state holiday celebrated on a different date in each state. The queen's birthday is celebrated in June, except in Western Australia, where it is celebrated in November

Recreation: Because of the mild climate, Australians who live near cities love to spend time outdoors visiting zoos, national parks, public gardens, and nature preserves.

Sports: Australians love sports. About one third of the people take active part in sports. Popular sports include swimming, surfing, fishing, sailing, bicycling, speedboating, and tennis. Popular team sports are rugby, soccer, and cricket. In winter, skiing and tobogganing are popular.

Communication: There are more than five hundred newspapers in Australia. The government operates the post office, telephone, and telgraph services. Australians send more telegrams per person than any other country in the world.

Transportation: The rail transit systems are run by the state governments. There are 25,000 mi. (40,200 km) of main-line railway. There are 510,000 mi. (821,000 km) of roads. Australia has about 70 ports and 400 airports. Some people who live in Sydney take boats or hydrofoils to work. (1982 statistics)

Schools: There are over 7,500 government schools, 2,200 private schools, 19 universities, and 10 medical schools. There are 3,000,000 schoolchildren and 160,000 full-time university students (1982). Many Australian children attend preschools. All children must start school at age six. At age fifteen a child may leave school and start working. In high school a student may study a variety of subjects, Australian schoolchildren have five days vacation at Easter, two weeks each in May and September, and six weeks from Christmas to February. Aboriginal children have bilingual education.

IMPORTANT DATES

 40,000-50,000 B.C. — Aboriginal tribes arrive in Australia
 150 B.C. — Greek philosopher, Ptolemy, predicts the existence of Australia and calls it *Terra Australis Incognita* (the Unknown Southern Land)
 A.D. 1606 — Captain Willem Jansz sights Australia
 1616-1619 — Dutch explore Australian coast
 1622-1629 — Dutch continue explorations of Australian coast
 1642 — Abel Janszoon Tasman sights Van Diemen's Land (Tasmania)
 1644 — Tasman explores the Gulf of Carpentaria
 1688 — William Dampier becomes the first Englishman to land in Australia
 1699 — Dampier explores Western Australia
 1768 — Captain Cook leaves England in *Endeavour* and sails to the South Pacific
 1770 — Captain Cook claims New South Wales for Great Britain

1779—Sir Joseph Banks decides to send British convicts to Australia
1788—British penal colony established in New South Wales; Sydney founded
1792—Australia begins trade with other countries
1793—First school opens in Sydney
1794—Captain Macarthur starts the sheep-breeding industry
1796—Matthew Flinders explores coastline aboard *Tom Thumb*
1797—Coal found in New South Wales
1801-1803—Matthew Flinders circumnavigates Australia
1802—Tasmania claimed for Great Britain
1813—G. W. Evans crosses the Blue Mountains
1815—Road built across the Blue Mountains
1824—Brisbane founded
1829—Captain Charles Fremantle claims Western Australia for Great Britain; Perth founded
1830—Captain Charles Sturt explores Australia's rivers
1835—Melbourne founded
1836—Adelaide founded
1839—Paul Strzelecki discovers gold in New South Wales
1840—Paul Strzelecki explores the Snowy Mountains and climbs Mount Kosciusko
1841—Edward John Eyre travels from South Australia to Western Australia
1844—Ludwig Leichhardt explores 2,000 mi. (3,219 km) of Australia from Brisbane to
the Gulf of Carpentaria
1845—Copper discovered in South Australia
1850—The first university established
1851—Gold discovered in New South Wales and Victoria
1855—Van Diemen's Land renamed Tasmania in honor of Abel Tasman
1862—John McDouall Stuart travels from the north of Australia to the south of Australia
1868—Great Britain stops sending convicts to Australia
1891—Australia's constitution is drafted
1894—Women receive the right to vote
1901—The Commonwealth of Australia formed
1914—Australia becomes involved in World War I
1915—Australian and New Zealand Army Corps (ANZAC) formed on April 25 (date
now celebrated as ANZAC Day)
1920—Qantas Airways founded
1923—Radio broadcasting begins
1925—Compulsory voting begins
1927—Canberra becomes the capital of Australia
1928—The Flying Doctor Service begins in Alice Springs
1930-1935—The Great Depression felt in Australia
1939—Australia joins in World War II
1952—Uranium ore discovered in South Australia and Northern Territory
1956—Television broadcasting begins
1963—Aboriginals given full rights as citizens
1967—Federal aid programs started for Aboriginals
1974—Cyclone strikes Darwin
1976—Aboriginal Land Rights Act passed
1981—Pitjantjatjara people given title to 40,000 sq. mi. (103,600 km^2) of land
1988—Australia celebrates its bicentennial
1989—Great Barrier Reef is in danger of destruction by swarms of starfish which
scientists believe to have increased in numbers due to destruction of natural predators
by commercial fishermen
1990—The worst brush fires since 1983 sweep New South Wales and North Victoria
killing thousands of head of sheep and other livestock and destroying over 125,000 acres
of land; the highest level of rainfall in 100 years causes severe flooding that covers more
than 500,00 square miles and damages over $10 million

IMPORTANT PEOPLE

Judith Anderson (born Frances Margaret Anderson) (1898-   ), actress, born in Adelaide, South Australia

John Antill (1904-   ), composer, born in Sydney, New South Wales

Joseph Banks (1743-1820), British naturalist who sailed with Captain Cook

Harold Blair (1924-   ), Aboriginal singer, born in Murgon

Evonne Goologong Cawley (1951-   ), Aboriginal tennis player, born in Barellan, New South Wales

Margaret Court (1942-   ), tennis player, born in Albury, New South Wales

James Cook (1728-1779), British captain who sighted Australia, named it New South Wales, and claimed it for Great Britain

William Dampier (1652-1715), British navigator who explored Australia

Edward Eyre (1815-1901), British explorer who explored wastelands of Australia

Matthew Flinders (1774-1814), British mariner who named Australia

Howard Walter Florey (1898-   ), Nobel Prize winner for codiscovering penicillin, born in Adelaide, South Australia

Errol Flynn (1909-1959), actor, born in Hobart, Tasmania

Mary Gilmore (1865-1962), poet and first woman member of Australian Workers' Union, born in New South Wales

Rodney Laver (1938-   ), tennis player, born in Rockhampton, Western Australia

Henry Lawson (1867-1922), writer, born in Grenfell, New South Wales

Ludwig Leichhardt (1813-1848), German explorer who traveled from Brisbane to the Gulf of Carpenteria

Frederick McCubbin (1855-1917), artist, born in Melbourne, Victoria

Nellie Melba (1861-1931), stage name of opera singer Helen Porter Mitchell, born in Melbourne, Victoria

Albert Namatjira (1902-1952), artist who became the first Aboriginal to be made a citizen, born in Northern Territory

John Newcombe (1944-   ), tennis player, born in Sydney, New South Wales

Andrew Barton (Banjo) Paterson (1864-1941), composer who wrote ''Waltzing Matilda,'' born in Narrambla, New South Wales

Arthur Phillip (1738-1814), British naval commander who founded New South Wales

Cyril Ritchard (1899-1977), actor, born in Sydney, New South Wales

Ken Rosewall (1934-   ), tennis player, born in Sydney, New South Wales

Carl Solander (1736-1782), Swedish botanist who sailed with Captain Cook

Arthur Streeton (1867-1943), artist, born in Victoria

Charles Sturt (1795-1869), British soldier who explored Australia's rivers

Joan Sutherland (1926-   ), opera singer, born in Sydney, New South Wales

Abel Janszoon Tasman (1603-1659), Dutch mariner who discovered Van Diemen's Land, now called Tasmania in his honor

Morris West (1916-   ), writer, born in St. Kilda, Victoria

Arthur Patrick White (1912-   ), writer and winner of the Nobel Prize, born in London of Australian parents

AUSTRALIAN PRIME MINISTERS

Name	Party	Dates Served
Edmund Barton	Protectionist	1901-1903
Alfred Deakin	Protectionist	1903-1904
John Christian Watson	Labor	1904
George H. Reid	Free Trade	1904-1905
Alfred Deakin	Protectionist	1905-1908
Andrew Fisher	Labor	1908-1909
Alfred Deakin	Fusion	1909-1910
Andrew Fisher	Labor	1910-1913
Joseph Cook	Liberal	1913-1914
Andrew Fisher	Labor	1914-1915
William M. Hughes	Labor	1915-1917
William M. Hughes	Nationalist	1917-1923
Stanley M. Bruce	Nationalist	1923-1929
James Scullin	Labor	1929-1932
Joseph A. Lyons	United	1932-1939
Earle Page	Country	1939
Robert G. Menzies	United	1939-1941
Arthur Fadden	Country	1941
John Curtin	Labor	1941-1945
Francis M. Forde	Labor	1945
Ben Chifley	Labor	1945-1949
Robert G. Menzies	Liberal	1949-1966
Harold E. Holt	Liberal	1966-1967
John McEwen	Country	1967-1968
John G. Gorton	Liberal	1968-1971
William McMahon	Liberal	1971-1972
Gough Whitlam	Labor	1972-1975
John Malcolm Fraser	Liberal	1975-1983
Robert James Lee Hawke	Labor	1983-

INDEX

Page numbers that appear in boldface type indicate illustrations

About the Author

Emilie Utteg Lepthien earned a BS and MA Degree and a certificate in school administration from Northwestern University. She has worked as an upper grade science and social studies teacher supervisor and a principal of an elementary and upper grade center for twenty years. Ms. Lepthien also has written and narrated science and social studies scripts for the Radio Council of the Chicago Board of Education.

Ms. Lepthien was awarded the American Educator's Medal by Freedoms Foundation. She is a member of the Delta Kappa Gamma Society International, Chicago Principals Association and life member of the NEA. She has been a co-author of primary social studies texts for Rand, McNally and Co. and an educational consultant for Encyclopaedia Britannica Films. Since she has traveled in Australia, writing about it was a natural for her.